FOREWORD

W hat's the blackest cloud in the sky over today's mega-church?

From this observer's perspective the biggest cloud is that sooner or later the senior pastor who led the building of that ministry will die, move away, retire, run off with the spouse of a member, be forced to resign, or simply depart because of a severe case of itchy feet.

My observations suggest that the departure of the senior minister after two decades or longer in serving what has become a very large congregation averaging more than 1500 at worship usually is followed by one of six scenarios. The most frequent is the new permanent successor arrives, and five years later worship attendance has dropped by 20 to 60 percent. A second and overlapping scenario is the minister who was expected to be the permanent successor becomes the unintentional interim senior minister and departs after one to three unhappy, tension-filled, and frustrating years.

A third and happier scenario develops when that minister who arrived expecting to be the permanent senior pastor quickly accepts the fact that reality demands first filling the role of the

PASSION + VISION=
TRANSFORMATION

The
Passion
Driven
Congregation

E. CARVER McGRIFF & M. KENT MILLARD

Abingdon Press
Nashville

THE PASSION DRIVEN CONGREGATION

Copyright © 2003 by Abingdon Press

All rights reserved.

This book is printed on acid-free paper.

Library of Congress Cataloging-in-Publication Data

McGriff, E. Carver, 1924-
   The passion driven congregation / E. Carver McGriff and M. Kent Millard.
      p. cm.
Includes bibliographical references.
   ISBN 0-687-02305-X (pbk. : alk. paper)
   1. Church growth—Methodit Church. 2. St. Luke's United Methodist Church (Indianapolis, Ind.) I. Millard, M. Kent, 1941- II. Title.

BX8349.C58M34 2003

254' 5—dc21

                                                                    2003002577

Scripture quotations, unless otherwise indicated, are from the *New Revised Standard Version of the Bible,* copyright © 1989, by the Division of Christian Education of the National Council of the Churches of Christ in the United States of America. Used by permission. All rights reserved.

Scripture quotations marked (GNT) are from the Good News Translation in Today's English Version-Second Edition © 1992 by American Bible Society. Used by Permission

04 05 06 07 08 09 10 11 12—10 9 8 7 6 5 4 3 2

MANUFACTURED IN THE UNITED STATES OF AMERICA

ACKNOWLEDGMENTS

There are so many, those splendid saints, the called ones: my friends, my colleagues in ministry, and most of all the people who made up that grand gathering called St. Luke's Church who shepherded me through tragedy and my often painful growing process and, at the last, allowed me to company with you to greatness. I presume to share the insights from your grace.

Perhaps I should put in words here my undying gratitude to Marianne. She, after all, surrounded me with love.

Thank you all.

E. Carver McGriff

I would like to express my deep appreciation to Bishop Woodie White, United Methodist Bishop of the Indiana Area, who took a "leap of faith" and appointed a little known pastor from South Dakota to lead the largest membership United Methodist congregation in the North Central Jurisdiction of The United Methodist Church. I thank God for the congregations I was privileged to serve in South Dakota (Flandreau-Egan, Rapid City Canyon Lake, Mitchell First, Sioux Falls First) and for the loving Dakotas laity and clergy who have nurtured me in my spiritual journey. I thank God for the outstanding laypeople and staff of St. Luke's United Methodist Church in Indianapolis who model what it means to be an open community of Christians who share God's love with all creation. Most of all, however, I thank God for Minnietta who is not only my loving wife but also my best friend, spiritual mentor, and leadership coach. God bless you all.

M. Kent Millard

CONTENTS

Foreword 9

Preface 15

Chapter 1 What *in the World* Is a Passion Driven Church? . . . 19

Chapter 2 Passion Inspired Leaders 43

Chapter 3 Successful Team Building 65

Chapter 4 Sunday at Eleven, and All Those

   Other Services 85

Chapter 5 Compassionate Change 109

Chapter 6 Heroes in the Sanctuary 129

Chapter 7 When It's Time to Leave: Smooth Transitions . . 149

Notes 167

unintentional interim senior minister. After ten to twenty months of effectively fulfilling that role, that person becomes his or her own successor and goes on to enjoy a creative and fulfilling decade or two or more as the senior minister.

A fourth and more intentional scenario begins with the decision to seek a trained and experienced intentional interim senior minister who has enjoyed at least one pastorate as the effective and productive senior minister of a very large congregation. "It worked because I knew the territory," explained one 67-year-old representative of this model. "Before retirement, I was the senior pastor of a congregation that averaged over 1800 at worship."

A fifth, and one of the most successful scenarios, calls for bringing the heir apparent on staff three to twelve years before the date of succession. That enables the future successor to understand the unique culture of that very large church, to earn the respect and support of both the volunteer leadership and the paid staff, to be mentored by the current senior minister, and to master the skills required "to do big church" effectively. While a growing number of very large congregations are choosing this scenario, nine out of ten do not. In several denominations it is either discouraged or unacceptable. When it works, that heir apparent often turns out to be the son or son-in-law of that long-tenured senior minister and thus brings no firsthand knowledge of any other congregational culture. A growing pattern in recent years begins with the twenty-eight-year-old associate minister who eventually is promoted to the position of senior associate and gradually assumes an ever increasing share of the responsibility for preaching before eventually being invited to become the successor.

This book describes a sixth scenario and what many believe is the ideal model. One reason it works is that this model requires a huge level of intentionality, a tremendous quantity of time, patience, prayer, and widespread support for evangelism and missions as central organizing principles. It also requires an affirmation that one of the big differences between the 1950s and the 1990s is the 1950s marked the end of an era in which great weight was given to functions such as administration, preaching, and teaching. In contemporary America far greater importance is attached to relationships.

Most critical of all is the relationship between the departing senior minister and the successor. Ideally a predecessor will be able and willing to mentor the successor. The successor will place a high value on that mentoring relationship. Both the predecessor and the successor must agree on the importance of continuity. The predecessor should leave a ministry plan and a legacy that the successor can authentically affirm, adopt, and own. The road to disaster is paved with declarations by the successor that the inherited ministry plan is, at best, irrelevant and must be replaced as quickly as possible. In the midsize congregation averaging 135 at worship, that is not a problem because one-half of the members ignore those declarations and the other half know this congregation is organized as a collection of small social networks, not around implementing someone's ministry plan.

Where does the leadership in the very large congregation find that ideal match between predecessor and successor? One alternative is to "raise our own" as described in that fifth scenario. More common today, however, is the national search. This requires those congregational leaders to be patient, to take advantage of the fact that distance is not the barrier it was in the 1950s, to be able to communicate accurately to each candidate the expectations they project, and to understand that an initial rejection may mean, "I'm not yet prepared to say yes," rather than to accept it as the final decision. (One of the roads to a mismatch comes when the prime candidate replies, "Yes, I'll be delighted to come and be your new senior minister," but the true message is, "I'll go anywhere to get out of the situation I'm in now!" That is one reason why the wise leaders define an initial rejection as, "Well, we've cleared one hurdle; this candidate may be the person we want.")

This book overflows with nuggets of wisdom and has several themes, but two messages stand out. The unique theme shows a textbook example of how to produce a happy and productive succession following the retirement of a long-tenured and exceptionally effective pastorate.

A second theme answers the question, "What will be the most important characteristics of the very large Protestant church in America in the twenty-first century?"

At the top of that list is the central theme of this book. The crucial characteristic is a contagious passion for the ministry of the worshiping community. The program staff and the volunteer leaders catch that contagious passion. That also is the key quality to look for in a successor.

A second characteristic is an obsession with quality. It is difficult to overstate the value of competence and quality. One example is that the demand for relevant and high quality preaching is at an all-time high in America.

A third characteristic is a profound understanding of the value of evangelism and missions in an ecclesiastical culture which tempts denominations and congregations to focus on choosing up sides over highly divisive and diversionary issues.

A fourth, which some will move up to second, is a sensitivity to the growing differences among people and an ability to offer creative responses that affirm those differences. One example in this book is found in chapter 4. Three of the ten weekly worship services at St. Luke's Church are offered four miles away at a second site called The Garden. The combined attendance at these three nontraditional worship experiences exceeds the weekly worship attendance of 99 percent of all the congregations in American Protestantism. That can be described as identifying a need and responding to it!

Two other important characteristics of the very large church in twenty-first century America are the program staff and the group life. The basic generalization is the larger the size of the congregation and/or the faster the rate of growth and/or the younger the age of the constituents, the more important are staff and group life. Both of those characteristics are described in this story.

Finally, if and when someone asks you to recommend a good book on the Protestant church in America in the twenty-first century, ask them to explain what they mean by the term, "good book." Do you mean you want a page-turner that is easy to read and grabs your interest? Or do you mean a book that is filled with earned optimism and hope? Or do you mean a book that affirms it is possible for one congregation to go beyond the rhetoric of being "inclusive" and translate that dream into reality? Or do you mean a book that provides realistic and workable guidelines about how to build a megachurch in the twenty-first century? Or do you want a book that is a dialogue rather than a monologue? Or are you looking for a book that is filled with practical wisdom about "how to do church in the twenty-first century?"

If the answer is, "All of the above," this is the book for you to recommend.

Lyle Schaller

PREFACE

Our purpose for this book is to provide encouragement, inspiration, guidance, and insight for local church pastors and lay leaders who are committed to renewing their local congregations for the sake of the transformation of the world. Many church leaders seem to assume that only theologically conservative congregations can grow, but the history of St. Luke's United Methodist Church in Indianapolis demonstrates that a passion driven, theologically progressive congregation can grow in numbers and depth over a long period of time. The vision of St. Luke's is to transform our society into a compassionate, inclusive, Christlike community, and we believe that the ultimate goal of all congregations ought to be to make a positive difference in the communities in which God has placed them.

When people ask me how St. Luke's came to be such a large and transforming congregation, I tell them it is because of the faithful and committed lay and clergy leadership over the long haul. St. Luke's was chartered on the second Sunday in March 1953, when a group of laypeople from Central Avenue Methodist Church organized to start a new congregation on the far north side of Indianapolis. They worshiped together for the first six

months without an appointed pastor until the Reverend Bill
Imler came as their first pastoral leader. He was followed six years
later by Dr. Dick Hamilton, who served for eight years, and then
Dr. Carver McGriff served St. Luke's for the next twenty-six
years. One of the primary reasons St. Luke's grew from 900 members
in 1968 to 4,000 members in 1993 is because Carver McGriff
chose to dedicate the vast majority of his pastoral service to one
congregation.

The formula for developing large and society-transforming
congregations is faithful competence over time. If a congregation
has competent and committed clergy and lay leadership over a
long time, it will grow. Unfortunately, most churches either have
competence for a brief time or incompetence over a long period
of time, and they therefore never reach their God-given potential.
In Carver McGriff, St. Luke's was blessed to have a very
competent, inspiring, and visionary leader over a long time and
therefore grew to become one of the largest United Methodist
congregations in the nation. In the normal course of church life,
St. Luke's would have had four or five senior pastors over a
twenty-six-year period and, if that had happened, would be today
a good 1,500-2,000-member congregation. Because Carver stayed
a long time and enrolled other long-term clergy and lay leaders,
St. Luke's became a congregation twice that size.

Also, in the normal course of church life, when a beloved,
long-term pastor retires, the next pastor is often a short-term
interim pastor. In fact, Dr. Lyle Schaller, the dean of church consultants
in this nation, predicted that I would be an "unintended
short-term interim pastor" because it so frequently happens that
way after an extended ministry by one pastoral leader. After I had
served at St. Luke's for several years, I saw Lyle Schaller at a conference;
and he asked why I wasn't the "unintended interim pastor"
that he had predicted. My immediate answer was that it was
because of the relationship between Carver and me.

When many pastors come to a new congregation they see
themselves as the savior of the church and their predecessor as
the "enemy" rather than as an ally. When I came to St. Luke's,
the first person I wanted to get to know was Carver McGriff

because I had genuine appreciation for anyone who could build a congregation from 900 members to over 4,000. Carver and I became friends and to this day, meet together for breakfast with other pastors twice a month. I saw Carver as a mentor, friend, and ally as we began to ask what God was calling St. Luke's to do next, and he has been most gracious both in his deeds and in his words of encouragement and support. I invited Carver back to preach at St. Luke's about a year after I came, and I explained to the congregation that Carver and I have exactly the same goal. He did not want to build a congregation from 900 to 4,000 members and then see all that he had built up decline after he retired. And I didn't want to come to a large congregation like this and see it fall apart after I came! We wanted to demonstrate that we both work together for the same God, and while our methods and procedures may differ on occasion, our goal is the same. Carver and I try to model collegiality in ministry by showing that God's work in the congregation is more important than either one of us and that our task is to work together in expanding God's ministry in this place.

St. Luke's is a passion driven congregation. Carver and I both have encouraged staff and laypeople to look inside at the spirit God has placed there and to discover the power, energy, and direction for their ministry. We believe that we are all made in the image of God, that there is a spark of God's spirit in every person, and that the role of the church is to help people discover that spark, fan it into flame, feed it, and watch God's spirit transform lives and situations. St. Luke's has a multitude of ministries from multiple work camp projects to spiritual formation classes to grief support groups, and all of these ministries have come from someone's passion.

Rick Warren, pastor of the Saddleback Valley Community Church in Orange County California, has written very helpfully about the "Purpose Driven Church" and enabled thousands of pastors and church leaders to focus on their purpose in ministry. Knowing your purpose in ministry is vital, but you also have to have a passion for it or you'll never achieve it. Purpose tells us where we are going, and passion gives us the energy to get there.

A person with a purpose and no passion will talk eloquently about a goal, but that goal will never be achieved. Ideally, a person and a church should be clear about their purpose and have an inner passion for it that will give them the energy and power to actually achieve it.

Carver and I decided to write this book in a dialogue form. Carver wrote the first part of each chapter sharing some of the wise principles that he used as lead pastor in the congregation. Then I wrote my reflections on the same topic showing how those principles have been maintained or modified as "new occasions teach new duties."

Carver and I love the local church, and each of us has had opportunities to serve in other non-local church responsibilities. However, we have each chosen to remain as local church pastors because we feel it is the front-line of Christian ministry and where most people have their most intense experiences of the power and presence of God. Our hope and prayer is that our reflections on local church ministry in one particular place will be helpful to other pastors and lay leaders in providing the leadership necessary for God to renew their congregations for the sake of transforming the society around them. May God bless our efforts.

M. Kent Millard

CHAPTER 1

WHAT *IN THE WORLD* IS A PASSION DRIVEN CHURCH?

E. CARVER McGRIFF

I n the Gospel of John we read that Jesus, after describing the commandments of God, said "I have told you this so that my joy may be in you and that your joy may be complete." Given the privation and suffering in the world, that's a powerful promise. Our churches are to be custodians of that message—and of that joy. Suffering and joy. Those are the components of the life Christ lived and to which he called us. A church that embodies those elements becomes a passionate church.

Merriam-Webster's Dictionary defines "passion" in several ways. "To suffer (as) the suffering of Christ on the cross." That's one definition. "Intense emotion compelling action." That's another.

"An emotion that stirs one to the depths of emotion, as love...."
That's still another. And so the "passion driven congregation" is
one moved to share the suffering of others, compelled to action,
and stirred to the depths by love. That kind of church can change
the world—and bring joy into the life of each individual who
enters. That kind of church deserves to grow.

Let's think about our beloved United Methodist Church. In
the year 2000 we suffered a net loss of 37,000 members. Lyle
Schaller reported that of those who "disappear" many move to
independent congregations, many move to other denominations
with more demanding membership expectations, and many simply leave without a paper trail by which to follow exactly where
they went. He reports that every year more than 100,000 discon-
tented United Methodist members follow what he terms this
"downhill, smooth, and attractive path." That is disaster in
process. In 1967 there were more than eleven million Methodists
in America. Now there are barely more than eight million
despite the country's continuing population growth. Schaller
estimates that the equivalent of two average congregations
"choose this scenario *every day*."[1]

True, there are a few extraordinary congregations showing
rapid and exciting growth, usually led by a highly gifted and
attractive leader. There are also an increasing number of vital,
growing congregations scattered across the country. But nationwide, we are in trouble and this need not happen. A great many
pastors and lay leaders of our congregations have the capability of
turning their congregations around and building them into growing, passionate congregations. Let's consider the inner workings
of such a church.

In what follows we are going to assume that we are praying
constantly for direction but prayers are not enough. We all know
Charlie Brown. One day we see him defending his snow fort.
Standing gallantly at his battlement, fist raised, he shouts his
heroic challenge to the world, declaring that he is invincible. No
one dares attack. Then suddenly, he is hit, *splat*, right in the back
of the head with a huge snowball. He turns around and sees Lucy
standing behind him with a self-satisfied smirk on her face.

Chagrined, Charlie lamely explains, "You'll notice that you had to use strategy, though, didn't you?"

That's what is needed now. Strategy. Kent Millard and I propose to share how St. Luke's United Methodist Church, at one time a small congregation located in the far north side of Indianapolis, grew to celebrate its fiftieth birthday with 5,000 members and more than 3,000 people worshiping in some ten worship venues each week. Despite a change of leadership, I after twenty-six years and Kent for the past ten years, the congregation has continued to thrive. Kent and I tried, by the grace of God and the assistance of a gifted lay leadership, to establish a foundation built on rock. The things we learned will work for you.

By 1967 some 300 people worshiped at St. Luke's on a typical Sunday. There was no brief period in the congregation's life during which meteoric growth took place. It happened steadily. Like many of your churches, St. Luke's was a stable, healthy small congregation. Then in the hectic era of the Civil Rights movement during which most congregations were in conflict, worship attendance rose to more than 600 even though this white suburban congregation was very much involved in the fray. During the Vietnam era as membership plummeted throughout the denomination and as "hawks" and "doves" were often at each other's throats in Methodist churches, St. Luke's attendance reached more than 1,000 despite the fact that three of her pastors took part in anti-war demonstrations in Washington. By the 1980s and the "me generation," 1,500 people worshiped at St. Luke's, and as the transition in pastoral leadership took place in 1993, attendance was nearing 2,000.

Kent Millard arrived to face a church whose pastor of twenty-six years had retired, leaving things in the hands of a much-loved young associate pastor, one whom many members hoped to see appointed as senior pastor. Conventional wisdom consigned Kent to a one-to-two-year interim pastorate, and it also consigned St. Luke's to a predictable drop in attendance. Conventional wisdom was wrong. The existing sanctuary was maxed out, but as soon as Kent led the congregation in the construction of a marvelous new sanctuary, with the advent of new and exciting ministries, attendance rose once more. Kent's vision and energy soon added other worship venues, and as of this writing, some 3,100 people now worship at St. Luke's each week. Despite some differences of personality and vision, Kent and I have employed essentially the same strategy in building this congregation, and it works. It will work in any church. What intrigues me as I write this is that most of Kent's innovations are as relevant to smaller, growing congregations as to the mega church, which St. Luke's has become.

One of the first things a pastor must decide is the answer to the question "What is a church?" That decision will determine the future for any congregation. I'm not thinking theologically for the moment, things like the body of Christ or the household of God. I'm thinking practically. What kind of organization does the busy visitor find when stopping by our place? Is there personal warmth here, a feeling of love free of judgment? If I'm a neophyte in the faith will I still feel welcome, that there's a place for me? If the church is to grow, it must start with that question—that, and the realization that as a parishioner I'm free to proceed at my own pace in deciding what I am willing and able to believe.

I would welcome everyone into my congregation. Old-time Methodists, of course. But so, too, homosexuals, divorced people, retired thieves, drug addicts, Presbyterians, struggling alcoholics, reforming prostitutes, and Sunday morning golfers welcome to my church. I encouraged my ordained colleagues to hold whatever theological beliefs they chose so long as those beliefs did not produce prudish judgmentalism. Deliver me from the kind of sour Christianity we see in some of today's churches where everyone is expected to toe someone else's theological line. From the day I stepped into the pulpit of St. Luke's Church I insisted that anyone who walks through our door is welcome as part of our family.

The story is told of a medieval peasant woman who met a Benedictine monk. She fell on her knees and begged, "Please tell me, holy father, what do you men of God do up there in the monastery on the hill? It appears to be so close to heaven. How do you spend your days and hours?" The monk pondered this for a bit then said, "I will tell you, my child. We fall down, we get up! We fall down, we get up!" There it is, the human dilemma. We're all in this together. Every one of us carries burdens of one sort or another. Every one of us conceals our sins, struggles with our failings, ponders our dreams. We all yearn to know the love that accepts us as we are without judgment. We all stand under conviction. We are all called to seek within ourselves to find that same unconditional love for others. We all find our hope in Jesus Christ.

We would all agree that the church is to try to be the embodiment of Jesus Christ, who loved every person he ever met. But we mustn't forget that to Jesus the number one sin was self-righteousness. "Judge not," he said, "lest you be judged by the measure with which you judge." In other words, hard-hearted people deserve a hard hearted God. Jesus hung out in bars, with prostitutes, and with the poor, the sick, and the lonely; and I presume many of them were in those conditions because of their dissolute lives. No matter. He loved them and wanted to save them. He did it by showing them acceptance and love. He laid it on thick enough when speaking in public. After all, the antidote to sin must be declared. But he'd turn around and show eternal patience to each individual. Think of the story where the young man approached Jesus and asked, "Master, what must I do to have eternal life?" We all know the story, and what always impresses me is the fact that when the young man sadly decided he could not comply with Jesus' advice and walked away, Jesus didn't call after him. He allowed him to walk away. I like the version in the tenth chapter of Mark's Gospel which includes this phrase: "Jesus looked at him with love…" I believe Jesus knew the fellow would be back, but the time wasn't right. Heavy-handed evangelism is a turnoff for me and for most people. Patient and persistent unconditional love nearly always wins. That's the church's job.

I believe that God is completely color-, ethnic-, language-, and culture-blind. To him a member of the Afghanistan Taliban is beloved just as I am. And this, by extension, applies to all people in my own society who are quite different from me, so I must take responsibility for a whole bunch of people whom I have never gotten to know very well. I may find this a darned nuisance, but I discover I am to become concerned about their welfare and I am to engage in whatever inner battles this may precipitate in order to help bring about this will of God. I will, of course, fail frequently. But my calling as a follower of Jesus is to try very hard to be this kind of person, to reach out at whatever expense to myself, in an effort to reveal as best I can the nature of God's love to those most in need. Missions—they're the work of the church. As theologian Emil Brunner said, "The church exists by missions as fire exists by burning." I have discovered that one great attraction a local church has for people is a strong mission outreach.

As for our theological beliefs, we can't allow any individual or group of individuals, however erudite and brilliant they may be or even how devout, to dictate final truths to any of us. Each of us must examine the evidence before us, the Bible first of all, the preaching of the church, and the counsel of people we have come to respect, and decide what is true for *me* and live by that. If this is done faithfully, I believe God will accept it. And need it be said, we won't all agree? John Wesley wrote in his *Advice to the People Called Methodist*, "Condemn no man for not thinking as you think: Let everyone enjoy the full and free liberty of thinking for himself; Let every man use his own judgment, since every man must give an account of himself to God."

Some of you may remember the old Kaufman and Hart play, *You Can't Take It With You.* The movie version stars Jimmy Stewart. For me it works as a metaphor for the church I'd want to attend. It is the story of a free-spirited family, the Sycamores, who live in New York City. Two old guys make fireworks in the basement, and occasionally they come up with singed eyebrows. A daughter is studying ballet and does her pirouettes in the living room, while the old man's daughter decides to write a novel because someone delivered a typewriter to her door by mistake. The mother is a sweet, flaky, but loving lady, while Grandpa, who opted out of the "rat race" because it "wasn't any fun," presides over this unconventional household and welcomes anyone who walks through the door. I forget all the other characters, except that they love anyone who comes to visit and are themselves totally uninhibited. Of course there's a love affair as strait-laced Jimmy Stewart falls in love with the other daughter, Jean Arthur, and is finally redeemed from his inhibitions. One reviewer, writing of this comedy, observed that its one serious note is that "most people are afraid to live their dreams."

There are four characteristics of that fascinating family which commend themselves to the church. The people all are free to be whoever they want to be; each accepts the other with all his or her eccentricities and without judgment; everyone is finding happiness in the relationships; and in the midst of this seeming chaos, two people find love. My hope is always that in that kind of church setting enough people would model Christian love that the rest would follow. That kind of welcoming, nonjudgmental openness characterizes for me the spirit of Jesus' teachings.

At St. Luke's we occasionally referred to that movie about those wonderful people as we walked the halls and heard the Jazzercise class yelling to its music, and saw the little kids from the preschool dashing down the hallway, while one of the many singing groups was belting out songs in the choir room. We each headed off to our various study groups to the clamor of arriving and departing parishioners and visitors wandering the halls. At night it was the shouts and banging of the volleyball games, the visiting barbershop quartet club rehearsing in the fellowship hall, the choir rehearsing in the sanctuary while down at the other end of the building quiet reigned as solemn folks shared their sadness in the grief recovery workshop. Starting Monday morning the parking lot was busy all week. Outside groups were welcome. We never allowed ourselves to feel inconvenienced as long as the church building was being used to serve and help people, members or not. My theory of church building ownership was this: give the place away. And you know what? New people, loving all the action, joined in large numbers. But this is important: St. Luke's in her fifty years of life has never grown by fewer than 100 members nor by as many as 200 members a year. It has been steady growth over the long haul.

One day in the summer of 1965, I heard a speech that changed my life as a pastor. It was delivered by Dr. Richard Myers, a church researcher employed by the Indianapolis Church Federation. Myers had chosen some thousand or more churches throughout America, churches of various Protestant denominations, and he had compiled their statistics, dividing the churches into three groups: growing, declining, and static. He then fed certain information about those churches into a computer and discovered that the growing churches had one important characteristic which the other two groups did not have. It was the proliferation of small, face-to-face groups of a wide variety, with a place for everyone, from the nursery on Sunday morning to the program for the elderly, and everyone is invited wherever they fit and want to be.

Myers discovered that, on average, each new small group would bring in seven new member families. He also found a direct correlation between worship attendance and the number of small groups, and as important as any factor, he found that a high percentage of people who teach church school classes are, themselves, involved in a small group in the church.

Psychotherapist Paul Tournier wrote of the dilemma of many people in a high-pressure, mechanized society this way:

> Most of our contemporaries, dragooned and drowned in our mass society, caught in the vortex of speed, find themselves isolated in unbelievable spiritual solitude. They have no one with whom to share their secret burdens. Everyone is in a hurry, caught in the superficiality of a mechanized society.[2]

Jesus spoke to this long ago: "And when two or three of you are together because of me, you can be sure that I'll be there." There's the human dilemma and the only really effective solution: small groups with Jesus present.

I was recently out of seminary when I heard Myers' presentation and had been assigned to start a new suburban church on the far east side of Indianapolis. At first the church had grown rapidly. After three years we had about 350 members with an attendance of perhaps 200 and had built a first sanctuary unit. But then we had plateaued. We also owned a half-completed house, which we used as a fellowship hall and which had an unused basement. The church school in our main building was full on Sundays.

After listening to Myers, I returned to my little congregation and urged the people to turn our unused basement into another church school. We divided the basement into five fairly good-sized rooms. We painted, furnished, and otherwise turned them into adequate school space, and within just a few weeks they were full. Myers was right. In the following year our attendance once more began to climb. We received a hundred new members, and attendance reached 270 in the following year. We could account for the increase in no other way but that the creation of five new church school classes, small groups, had caused us to begin growing again.

Many pastors of growing churches are often too busy to visit their church schools to see how crowded things really are, and these are our most important small groups. Studies have shown that only a certain number of children of each age can exist comfortably for the better part of an hour in a room of given size with one or two teachers. So let's suppose you discover that your class of five-year-olds is full at your 9:30 service. If, the next Sunday, a new family arrives with a five-year-old child, the family is, in effect, told, "We don't have a place for you in our church." Either their five-year-old will be unhappy and they will seek another church or they will force their five-year-old to continue in that room and some other five-year-old child will then become unhappy and his or her parents will leave the church. Or you'll soon have five-year-olds wiggling unhappily in your worship service. *Take a Sunday off from the pulpit and wander the halls of the church school, see what's going on. It's there that the future of your congregation is being determined.*

Sometimes, when things are static in a church and there don't seem to be enough teachers, the church school director will double up, putting first- and second-graders together, for example. That's a sure path to a no-growth situation. There's a tremendous difference between first and second grade. First-graders are often just learning to read while second-graders are doing rather well at that. A second-grader's added year's growth usually leads to socialization well advanced of the new first-grader. This can be very intimidating to the first-grader who may very well have such a fit at going to Sunday school that Mom and Dad either start looking for another church or, if it's a small community with no other options, they may take the child to church with them, which means the child misses all the socialization and faith learning to be had in a good church school. Either that happens or the teacher gears everything to the first-graders, and the second-graders get bored. Either way growth is impossible.

Now let's consider another source of small groups, one which is right under our noses. I mean the committees and commissions which compose our church body. We all know, of course, that they are small groups. Very small in many cases. There is too often a reason for that. Church business meetings are often boring. Or worse, meetings are either canceled or meeting times are changed to fit someone's schedule. Who among us has not structured our day so we could attend a meeting only to receive a late call that "since there's nothing important to talk about we're going to cancel?" Sometimes it's to accommodate the pastor, a grievous mistake. A good committee should function perfectly well without a minister being present. Pastors who insist on always being present at these meetings can easily thwart true leadership by causing otherwise good leaders to defer to the "expert" who, in all too many situations, knows less than others in the room about the subject under discussion. If effective lay leaders are to step up and really lead, it will usually be by virtue of the pastor's willingness to stand aside and trust them enough to let it happen. Otherwise, pretty soon the chairperson and one or two other influential members make all the decisions. Disinterested members, pleased not to have another lengthy meeting anyway, are happy to have an unexpected free evening, and they remain uninformed, not to mention disinterested. I plead guilty in my early years of viewing some of the working groups of the church as nuisances to be endured.

Whose fault is this? In my church it was my fault. For a long time in ministry I had the very limited idea that the main function of the finance committee, for example, was to oversee the finances of our church. When the chair of the stewardship committee told me they had decided to disband since the finance committee made all the financial decisions, I was glad to have one less group to worry about.

One day a man whose work I respected pointed out to me the error of my ways. He showed me that the main function of a finance committee is to bring people together in the name of Jesus Christ to spend time together in Christian fellowship, to become friends, and while there, to oversee the finances of the church. Even though there may not be any financial business this month, there is equally important business: being together with fellow Christians. What if an individual, agreeing to serve on the finance committee, also agreed to be there as a member of the body of Christ, to share in the friendship of people who care about that body, who are willing to pray for each other and the church, and who make room in their hearts for these new friends in Christ? What if we emphasized to people who agree to serve on one of the church's management groups that they are making a solemn commitment to participate on a regular basis? It's amazing how many financial types secretly yearn for new relationships based on such cleansing, healing terms. Every one of us is searching, deep down, for hope, what one poet defined as "the belief that joy is coming soon." I realized that when I attend a meeting, no matter how mundane the topic, every person entering that room is hoping for something that only Jesus Christ can provide and that there, in that room, he is there as we gather in his name. It is the same for the other committees of the church.

One problem most smaller churches must confront as growth takes place is the tendency of many church members to feel proprietorial about building facilities. We faced this in the early days at St. Luke's one week when the United Methodist Women had scheduled a meeting to which a special invitation was issued to the congregation's women members, this having been scheduled on the same date and at approximately the same time as I had scheduled a meeting to convene a new women's daytime book study group. The president of the United Methodist Women was very angry with me and insisted that my meeting potentially would pull attendees from her meeting. She felt that I should reschedule my meeting, as hers seemed more important to the women of the church. Thus was raised one of the most controversial strategic problems facing a growing congregation: Should organizations within the congregation compete for members?

There are, of course, certain battles it is best not to win, and I acceded to my friend's wishes and rescheduled my meeting. But the larger issue was before us, and at the next meeting of our ad board I presented the following equation. Suppose a group like the UMW has planned a meeting and, say, twenty-five women will attend. Suppose, further, that to protect this very important occasion, nothing else is scheduled which might interfere. No doubt a very valuable experience will be had by all at that meeting, and twenty-five people will have been served. But now let's suppose a different approach. The pastor also schedules a study-group meeting, ten women attend, but attendance at the UMW is only twenty women. Yes, in the short run, five attendees were lost to that UMW meeting. But a total of thirty women were served by their church that day. Those five women who chose the study group instead of the UMW meeting had been presented with a larger choice of ministries, had found one that better met their particular needs, and the total number of people served on that occasion had increased by twenty percent. The church had, ergo, grown.

To generalize, the point must come in the life of a congregation where multiple programming is encouraged and an ever widening assortment of options is offered to meet the needs of the people, even though there will be times when offerings seem to conflict. In our case, the long-term effect of our decision to encourage multiple offerings at any given time was the doubling of the size of the UMW meetings after a very few years, as well as the proliferation of a variety of missions, ministries, and services for our people. However, the wise pastor doesn't just push forward with this idea. Leaders of the congregation must first understand and agree with the wisdom of this policy. There may be some confusion, an occasional misfire in the early going, but the more freedom felt by various leaders to schedule worthwhile activities despite such scheduling conflicts, the more open and varied the life of the congregation will become.

Study groups using the Bible or other appropriate literature can do wonders for a church—and for people. I remember most fondly the day a group of us friends were sitting in my front yard many years ago, discussing the fact that we were all members of the Methodist Church but we didn't know much about the Bible or our faith. We agreed to form a study group. We would meet as families in homes twice a month, and we would start with Matthew and also read books by various authors of the day. Our senior pastor met with us for a few sessions, then pushed us out into deep water. We would take turns leading discussions. We would start on time and end on time. We would have refreshments but never anything so lavish as to start a little competition among our hosts. This was where I found Jesus Christ. Or to be more precise, where he found me. In the years that followed, everyone in that group moved from a cursory interest in the faith to a devout acceptance of Christ. When Jesus assured us that when two or three are gathered together in his name he would be there, he certainly kept his word in our case. Of course he will in every case. And each small group has the potential to change lives, energize a church, and make a difference in the world.

Still another opportunity for small group activity is in our mission outreach. An optometrist in St. Luke's Church became interested in a small, poverty-ridden community in the south of the Island of Jamaica. He first visited them and fell in love with the people. Out of that love on his part there have, so far, been three work projects there involving more than twenty people each time. The trips were about ten or twelve days in duration, and I can witness, having gone twice, that deep and lasting friendships are made when people wield hammer and nails together. I suppose, in the event some of those people should read these words, I should confess I was worth very little when the work was being done. But in a way that's my point. There's room for everyone on one of those projects. The same is true for Habitat For Humanity projects and, in fact, for the myriad of caring ventures undertaken by all our churches. God, as we know, blesses those who give and those who receive.

Many pastors believe in devoting a lot of energy to going out into the community, house to house, in an effort to bring people into their churches. I think this is usually a waste of effort. If someone were to throw a handful of iron filings on the floor and ask you to retrieve them, you would be there a long time if you tried to do it with a pair of tweezers. If you used a magnet, you'd have them in no time. The same is true of people. My emphasis would be twofold: concentrate on the very strongest possible programming in your church and urge church members to bring their friends. Give your church a local reputation for excellence. I think we could say you want your church to become the talk of the town for Jesus' sake.

Look for opportunities to invite your larger community into your building. Make it available for musical and other groups that are appropriate and can bless the people in one way or another. Welcome community groups. Let people become familiar with your facilities and your people. Be sure your own members are friendly when non-members arrive for these events. This all contributes to a welcoming, cordial atmosphere; and when the time finally comes that a person is ready to seek the answers, your church will come to mind.

If I were to visit your church on a weekday, would I easily be able to find my way to your office? How many times have you driven to an unfamiliar church then walked around from door to door trying to find your way in? Be sure your church conveys an atmosphere of welcome from the moment a visitor drives onto your property. A sign directing the visitor to the main entrance is a great help. Once I find my way in, can I easily find my way to the office or elsewhere if I'm attending a meeting? Older buildings can be especially confusing with their narrow hallways and faceless doorways, sometimes numbered, but with numbers which mean nothing to the visitor. One excellent investment for any congregation is to place signs that clearly show the visitor the way. One church in our community made such an investment several years ago, and to visit there is a pleasure simply to see the colorful, friendly signs that enable a visitor to easily navigate the otherwise impenetrable maze of multistoried halls and cornered turns. Take a few minutes, pretend you are new and unfamiliar with the way, visit your own church on behalf of all the other people soon to visit, be sure the way is clear and conveys a friendly welcome.

What about on Sunday morning? If I'm a visitor, will someone show me how to find my child's classroom? Will I receive a welcoming call shortly thereafter? If I decide to join, will I later be invited to work and fellowship in some area of the church's life?

I once visited a large church that employed several women volunteers who, wearing pink smocks as identification, wandered the building on weekdays with the express purpose of greeting members and outsiders alike with friendly smiles and offers to help them find their way. It was my first visit there, but I came away with a warm feeling that I was welcome and my mission was important. I firmly encourage some version of this practice for every church. Just a few people with outgoing personalities can do wonders for any congregation.

A church building should belong to the community. The more you give it away, the more it is truly yours. I used to ask new members in our membership classes what brought them to St. Luke's. I was surprised at how many said they had been a bridesmaid or a groomsman in some wedding we had done and that everyone was so friendly and cooperative they decided to try us on Sunday morning. Surely God doesn't enable us to build grand buildings with the thought that we'd then set up some rather limiting restrictions on their use. If everything we do is, at heart, to win people to Christ, then the building itself exists for that reason. And we win people by surrounding them with practical, life-ministering, life-changing love.

Bring people in for any reason, treat them as you would a guest in your home, and train office personnel to do the same. We made it clear to anyone seeking a position as a secretary in our office that if it's going to drive you up a wall to have constant interruptions by various church members and visitors, then you won't be happy here.

Recently in my community, a growing church discovered that, as a new school year was to begin, their preschool program had outgrown its building and they needed more space. They approached the local Presbyterian church and asked if they might rent a classroom for the coming year. The pastor, after discussing this request with his trustees, is said to have responded to the request this way: "No, we can't possibly rent the space to you. We will, however, invite you to use it at no cost." That's my kind of church. If I had my way, churches would never charge worthy outside groups for access to their facilities. I'm pretty sure that attitude brings in more people—and more money—than will running a church like a small business.

Professor Robert Putnam of Harvard in his studies of society's problems referred to "Social Capital" as the combined energy available for creative and constructive living. The dust jacket of his book, *Bowling Alone*, states:

> Communities with less Social Capital have lower educational performance and more teen pregnancy, child suicide, low birth weight, and prenatal mortality. Social Capital is also a prime predictor of crime rates and other measures of neighborhood quality of life, as it is of our health.[3]

By Social Capital, Putnam is describing the spiritual and intellectual interactions of people in community. *He discovered that the best source of this capital is the local church.*

"Regular worshipers," he writes,

> are much more likely than other people to attend club meetings, and to belong to sports groups; professional and academic societies; school service groups, youth groups; service clubs; hobby or garden clubs; literary, art, discussion and study groups; school fraternities and sororities; farm organizations, political clubs; nationality groups.[4]

In other words our churches are the prime contributors to that Social Capital which builds strong, healthy communities. Our church is not only the source of God's communication with us through Jesus Christ, it is the locus of a very practical ministry to the world in which we live.

I'm aware that sometimes trustees and finance committee people have other ideas having to do with wear and tear on the carpet, the cost of heat and light for outsiders, and the horrifying thought that people who have never paid a dime in support of the church are enjoying its facilities as much as are the members of the church. So, I always made it a point to see that a few members of those groups were people who saw things my way. I also pointed out that if the average family contributes, say, fifteen hundred dollars a year to the church and we were to get one new member family because of this policy then, presto, we've paid for a lot of heat and light.

Reflections on Chapter 1

M . KENT MILLARD

In chapter 1 Carver has described the unique character of St. Luke's United Methodist Church. That special character is described in our church's mission statement which says: "St. Luke's is an open community of Christians who gather to seek, celebrate, live, and share the love of God for all creation." This mission statement was developed by the leaders of the congregation about fifteen years ago and is engraved on a brass plaque outside the original sanctuary, illustrated in a large stained-glass window in the new narthex, and printed on the weekly bulletin and in all publications. However, it is not just printed in various places but is the functional principal, which influences all of our decisions.

When I first came to visit St. Luke's in 1993 and saw the mission statement on the brass plaque, something within me said, "Yes! I would like to be a part of an open congregation of Christians like this." We are an open community of Christians because Jesus was an open embodiment of the unconditional love of God. Jesus opened his arms and his heart to all sorts and conditions of people; prostitutes, tax collectors, lepers, beggars, and all others who were rejected by the religious leaders of his day. In fact his major critics, the Pharisees, once saw that Jesus was eating with those whom they would reject, and they criticized him saying, "Why does he eat with tax collectors and sinners?" (Mark 2:16). Furthermore, when Jesus allowed a "woman of the streets" to wash his feet with her tears and to dry them with her hair he was criticized by a Pharisee for allowing such a person to touch him. Jesus scolded the Pharisee for his hardness of heart and said: "I tell you, her sins, which were many, have been forgiven" (Luke 7:47). Jesus was characterized by his openness, forgiveness, and inclusiveness, and we believe that a congregation that is faithful to Jesus will be equally open, forgiving, and inclusive of all people.

35

The United Methodist Church has developed a nationwide publicity campaign with the slogan: "Open Hearts, Open Minds, Open Doors—The People of The United Methodist Church." As a denomination, we seek to be a church that has an open mind when it comes to listening and learning about what God is trying to teach us through others. We have open hearts as we reach out to feed the hungry, clothe the naked, house the homeless, and care for people in need all around the world. And we have an open door at the church where everyone is welcome to enter and experience the unconditional love of God, which comes to us in Jesus Christ.

St. Luke's congregation has sought to live up to that mission throughout its fifty years of existence. It is a congregation that is open to persons of all races, genders, lifestyles, and theological positions. For example, there is a large group of gay and lesbian persons who are actively involved in the worship and ministry of St. Luke's, and there are also many people at St. Luke's who have been a part of the Promise Keepers movement and who participate in Emmaus Walk retreats. We host city-wide services welcoming gay and lesbian persons and their families, and we regularly host Emmaus retreats for persons who seek to experience the unconditional love of God through a weekend retreat. We believe that being open means including persons with a wide variety of theological opinions on many of the significant issues facing the church today. We seek to follow John Wesley's words when he said, "Though we may not think alike, may we not love alike?"

We also keep reminding ourselves that Jesus once said: "Do not judge, so that you may not be judged. For with the judgment you make you will be judged and the measure you give will be the measure you get. Why do you see the speck in your neighbor's eye but do not notice the log in your own eye?" (Matthew 7:1-3). We believe we are called not to judge each other but to love each other. It is God's prerogative to judge, and all of us will ultimately be held accountable to God for what we have or have not done with the gift of life we've been given, but it is not our role to judge one another. Jesus made it abundantly clear that we are called to love God with our whole being and to love our neighbor as ourselves—"that is the essence of all the law and the prophets" (Matthew 22:40).

On many Sunday mornings there is a whole row of young men who are gay who come to worship together at St. Luke's. At the end of the services they would stand and greet the people in the pew behind them and became well acquainted with an elderly couple who usually sat there. One day the wife of that elderly couple said to one of the young men: "It is so nice to see you young men worshiping together. Are you a baseball team?" The young man responded by saying, "No, we're not a baseball team; we're just good friends, and we feel welcome here." It's a joy to be a part of an open congregation where Christ's love is shared with everyone regardless of their race, creed, gender, or sexual orientation.

One day a fairly conservative pastor in our community challenged me about welcoming gay people in our services. He said, "When they come, are you changing them?" I responded by telling him that we don't change anybody; God is the only one who changes people. We simply bear witness to the unconditional love of God, which comes to us in Jesus Christ; and God does all the changing necessary in their lives and the lives of all of us who surrender ourselves into God's hands. We humans seem to want to play the role of God in order to change people into our image, rather than simply loving them and allowing God to transform us all into God's image.

We have tried to model this openness and diversity of theological opinion on our church staff. For example, we have one pastor on our staff who believes that homosexuality is a sin, that it is not what God intended in creation. However, he would go on to say that he too is also a sinner and as God is the judge of all, it is not his responsibility to judge another's sin. Another pastor on our staff believes homosexuality is not a sin. She believes that it is not a choice and that if it's not a choice, how can it be a sin? While these two pastors think very differently about this important theological and social issue, they do love and respect each other and work well together. They model for all of us what the church of Jesus Christ should be: a place where we may not all think alike, but we can all love alike and allow God's love to flow in and through us into the lives of those around us.

The openness of St. Luke's was demonstrated after the tragic terrorist attack on September 11, 2001 in New York City, Washington D.C., and in Pennsylvania. We opened our doors to the community and more than 5,000 people came to our special worship services where we grieved with all those who lost loved ones, re-evaluated our priorities in life, affirmed our belief in eternal life, and prayed for justice and peace in our world. While in many places this increased attendance after 9/11 dropped off shortly thereafter, the increase in worship attendance has continued at St. Luke's since September 11, 2001. Our average attendance increased by 25 percent from September through December, 2001, with six hundred more people per Sunday than in the same period the previous year. Furthermore, many of those who first came after the terrorist attack have continued to attend services, have become involved in the ministries of the congregation, and many have joined the church. After services on September 16, 2001, a member of our congregation introduced herself to a gentleman in the pew beside her and asked if he regularly attended St. Luke's. He responded by saying, "I have never attended church before in my life." She asked why he came that Sunday, and he explained that he felt so empty that he had to come someplace to try to make sense of what had happened. I believe that many of the people who came after 9/11 have continued to attend because they experienced an open community of Christians who welcomed them, and they felt the living presence of God in the worship services.

In the weeks that followed, we had classes on Islam, invited Muslim and Jewish leaders to speak from our pulpit, and participated in numerous interfaith dialogues to help create a better climate of mutual understanding and respect among people from all religious traditions. It was also a time for us to remember that there are self-righteous, violent terrorists in all of our religious traditions. We have self-righteous, violent terrorists out of the Christian tradition who call themselves the Ku Klux Klan, or the militia, or the White Supremacy movements. We have self-righteous violent terrorists out of the Jewish faith who assassinated an Israeli Prime Minister, and we also have violent self-righteous terrorists out of the Muslim faith who committed the terrorist acts on September 11. We all need to be open to acknowledging our own sins when it comes to terrorism committed in the name of our religious traditions.

Many church leaders seem to believe that it is only theologically conservative congregations that are growing; however, St. Luke's has demonstrated for the past fifty years that a theologically progressive congregation that is open and inclusive of all persons can also grow in size, in spirit, and in outreach. I believe God will bless any congregation that opens its doors and heart to all and models God's unconditional love revealed in Jesus Christ.

I am a passionate, compassionate, visionary, loving, Christian leader, and my vision is to renew the church for the sake of the transformation of the world. It is obvious that our world needs to be transformed from a culture consumed with greed to a community committed to generosity and from a system sick with self-centeredness to a society centered on compassion. Corporate greed, dishonesty in high places, casual sex, racial prejudice, terrorism, hatred, war, and lack of personal integrity are all characteristics of contemporary society that are destroying our human community. Political, professional, educational, business, and religious leaders all bemoan the current direction of our society but seem impotent to transform it or turn it around.

It used to be that we looked to the government to solve all the ills of our society. While government has an important role to play in maintaining peace and justice in our communities, it has become clear in recent years that the government cannot bring about inner spiritual changes, which are needed to transform people and to turn our society around. For a while we believed our educational institutions would be the vehicle for transforming our world. We believed that if everyone got a good education, our world would be changed, but we have discovered that education without ethics and morality does not bring about the changes needed. Business institutions have an important role in providing the resources we need for living, but corporate greed and corruption have disillusioned us regarding the capacity of the business community to model and bring about these needed inner changes.

I am convinced the local congregation is the primary institution in our communities through which God can transform our world into a compassionate and inclusive community. It seems that transformation is coming not through denominational structures or national boards and agencies but through local congregations who are surrendered to God and committed to loving service in their communities and beyond.

Jesus once called his twelve apostles together and filled them with power and authority to go out and transform the world around them. Jesus gave his followers power to cast out unclean spirits and demons (Luke 9:1-6). I believe that Jesus continues to give us the power to cast out the unclean spirits that plague us: pride, ego, greed, and prejudice. Jesus also sent his followers out to proclaim the good news that God is present in every moment and every place of life, which is what is meant by the phrase "the kingdom of God is at hand." The local church is where people can continue to experience the living presence of God; experience Christ's healing in body, mind, emotions, relationships, and soul; and are sent out to transform the world around them.

The vision of St. Luke's United Methodist Church is that the world around us would become more compassionate and less judgmental; more inclusive and Christlike and less exclusive; and less centered on egoism, control, and power.

The goal of St. Luke's is not simply to become an increasingly larger congregation. It is not about how many people come to the church but about how many people go from the church to transform the society around them that matters. If the Indianapolis community in which we live is not a better place because of us, then we have failed to fulfill the vision to which God has called us. If the world is not a better place because of us, then we have let down our Lord. Jesus called his twelve apostles together, filled them with his power and his love not simply for their own personal edification and inspiration but to send them out to transform the lives of those around them. In a similar way, Christ continues to call us together, and fill us full to overflowing with his power and his love; not so that we can boast of his presence in our lives, but so that he can use us in the transformation of our world.

The United Methodist Church has declared that our mission is to "make disciples," which comes from the Christ's statement in Matthew 28:19. A disciple is one who comes to learn from a teacher, and we are to teach people the ways of God following the example of our master teacher, Jesus Christ. However, I believe the above mission statement is incomplete. The Gospels refer to the twelve closest followers of Jesus as "apostles," and the word apostle means "one who is sent." Jesus believed that his followers should not only come to him as "disciples" (learners) but that they were also to be sent out as "apostles" (missionaries) to transform the world with the good news. Our mission may be to make disciples, but our ultimate vision is to make apostles who have been filled with the power and love of God and who are sent out to transform our world. We pray for this transformation every time we pray the Lord's prayer saying, "Thy kingdom come on earth as it is in heaven." Jesus taught us to pray for transformation "on earth;" that is, in the world around us.

While we are a long way from the fulfillment of this vision, God is using St. Luke's to transform race relations in our community through our partnering with three inner-city African American congregations in providing volunteers for tutoring and mentoring programs in inner city schools, meals for homeless and low-income families, interracial study circles to help us recognize the problems caused by white privilege, and through participation with forty other congregations in a movement to build bridges of understanding and respect across racial and denominational barriers. God has also led us to model this inclusiveness by the leadership of an African American woman pastor on our staff for the first time in the history of our congregation.

St. Luke's is also seeking to be a channel of transformation in society by sending out three hundred youth and adults each year to work on projects in our community and around the world, by providing the funds and labor to build at least one Habitat for Humanity house each year in our community, and by giving away nearly half a million dollars each year in support of mission projects.

In order to help transform the youth culture around us, St. Luke's initiated a partnership with ten other congregations in establishing a Youth Coffeehouse in a large shopping center. Young people now have an alcohol-free, smoke-free environment with concerts of positive music where they can hang out. We have also started a satellite congregation in a dinner theatre, which is transforming the lives of more than a thousand people, seventy percent of whom had no previous church experience prior to coming to The Garden. We will discuss the establishment of this satellite service more completely when we discuss our multiple worship services in chapter 4.

We believe that God has raised up every congregation in every community to be a transforming presence in that community. John's Gospel tells us that God so loved the world that he sent his only son so that the world might be saved through him (John 3:16-17). Every congregation should assess where the human needs and pains are in its community and seek God's guidance in mobilizing to meet those needs with the good news of Jesus Christ, who has commissioned us to transform the lives of all those around us.

While our motivation is to allow God to use us in the transformation of the world, one of the byproducts of reaching out to be a positive influence in the community is that the congregation will grow in spiritual depth and in numbers. Our experience has been that many people want to be a part of a faith community that is making a positive difference in the world and will grow in their own faith as they share God's unconditional love with people in need around them.

CHAPTER 2

PASSION INSPIRED LEADERS

E. CARVER MCGRIFF

The church belongs to its members, and the truly compassionate congregation will always be one in which the laity are its primary ministers. Empowerment of lay members is the most important work of the pastor and the professional team members. When Paul said, "We are ambassadors for Christ, since God is making his appeal through us (2 Corinthians 5:20)," he was referring to the rank and file of us Christ followers. So first, what about the presiding pastor? What kind of person can best lead us? What qualities make for an effective leader?

First, an effective senior pastor must have vision, the ability to foresee events and opportunities with a high degree of accuracy. A wise man once wrote, "A blind man's world is bounded by the limits of his touch; an ignorant man's world is bounded by the limits of his knowledge; a great man's world by the limits of his vision."

Stephen R. Covey in his excellent *The Seven Habits of Highly Effective People* uses the image of a group of people slogging their way through an almost impenetrable jungle. At the very front are those with machetes, heroically hacking their way ahead of the rest. Behind them are the people who sharpen the machetes as they become dulled by the heavy undergrowth. Covey identifies these machete wielders as the *producers* or problem solvers, cutting their way into the future, with the *managers* there behind them, supplying them with the means to do their work effectively.[1]

Many clergy see themselves as the managers, responsible for enabling the congregation to do the extended work of ministry. Both the people in great numbers doing the work of the Lord (producers) and the clergy who motivate and empower this work (managers) are essential to the Christian experience.

But what about the leader? Covey, in his image, also supposes yet another participant, someone sitting high up in a nearby tree. There's your leader, sitting quietly, able to survey the distant scene, calling down "a little to your right if you please" (or, as Covey suggests, "wrong jungle"). The responsibility of the leader is clearly different from that of the manager. The effective pastor-leader of a large and growing church must be different from the traditional role of a pastor. The pastor-leader must have additional qualities. It seems to me that there are some obvious characteristics of people who have that sense of where we ought to go next and how we can get there.

One: A visionary person takes time for quiet thoughtfulness. This may be done in a private office. It may also be done on a bicycle, on a long distance run, while pacing the floor of one's study at home, or while quietly eating a bite of lunch in an out-of-the-way cafe. Once in a while, a two- or three-day retreat is also a good idea. Somehow, time must be spent in thoughtful meditation on the mission at hand.

Two: A visionary person spends time with people. This means with both those of strong faith, and as important, with people outside the faith, interacting, noting their points of view, hearing their perceptions about current events. Talk with other pastors, especially those who seem to be innovative, far-seeing leaders themselves. If you are young and early in your ministry, call that pastor whom you have come to admire, someone who is leading the way in ministry, and ask to have lunch together. I know of several such people, and every one would be more than delighted to respond to such an invitation with a hearty "Yes!" Listen to them. Become a friend to them.

Three: A visionary person stays in touch with the real world. Go to current movies, the ones people are talking about. Travel extensively. Attend parties. Break down the natural discomfort many people feel when speaking with clergy. I don't mean cultivate disrespect, but don't be afraid for people to know you.

Four: A visionary person reads. Obviously, there are too many books for one person to read, so listen to the people you respect, find out what they're reading, and perhaps take part in an organized discussion group. Be aware too that most religious books are written by introverted, scholarly people, so be sure to seek out books and articles by people struggling in the heat of the day as well. However, and this is a major pitfall for many clergy, don't sway with every wind. Don't latch on to every new idea and run off to success at last. How many young clergy are ardent fans of this or that new guru? Read articles from viewpoints other than your own. Be sure, too, to read periodicals from the business and professional arenas. Some understanding about the economic scene and international relations will suggest what tomorrow may hold. A true visionary is out in front, creating, thinking ahead, leading.

Five: A visionary person refuses to get bogged down in the minutiae of the everyday. It's easy to become preoccupied with the details of life to the point that we lose perspective of our goals. Think of that fellow sitting in the tree. I'm not for a moment commending laziness. I am, however, commending the kind of exertion that may not be visible to other people. Victor Hugo, a prolific author, wrote, "A man is not idle because he is absorbed in thought.

There is a visible labor and there is an invisible labor. Thought is the labor of the intellect."

Six: A visionary person spends time with the leaders of the congregation. We all know that there are certain people in our churches whose words determine the decisions of the various committees and boards that run the place. The more those people become your friends and the more you know what and how they think, the more effectively you will be able to persuade them of your vision for their church. For several years I led bicycle trips through foreign countries. Many of my congregation's young leaders came along. We struggled up mountain passes, rode all day in frigid rains, slept in dingy little inns, and had a great time sitting around some dinner table after a hard day's ride laughing, joking, then trudging up to bed so we could do the whole thing again the next day. We learned to trust each other.

First, go into the other person's world. Most church members come to your world on Sunday or to those meetings we discussed. The wise pastor goes where the people spend their days. At St. Luke's I learned that business people consider lunch to be the best place to talk and get acquainted and that they should be the one to pick the place. Time spent in these ways is well invested.

Second, an effective senior pastor is comfortable with stress. A number of years ago Bruce Larson accepted a Lilly Foundation grant to do research into the question, "What constitutes a healthy minded person?" He interviewed leaders in the mental health field, people like Paul Tournier in Switzerland and Karl Menninger of the famous clinic. He asked that question and received a variety of answers, but he reported that the one characteristic mentioned by every professional person interviewed was that a healthy-minded person is a *risk taker*.[2] To be healthy in the world requires the ability, perhaps even the courting, of stress. Kierkegaard said it well: "Without risk faith is an impossibility."

John Maxwell told of watching Mike Wallace interview a Sherpa guide from Mount Everest. Thinking of the incredibly stressful work the man did, he asked him, "Why do you do it?" The Sherpa replied, "To help others do something they can't do themselves." Wallace then asked the man how he can bring himself to face the extraordinary risks day after day. The Sherpa replied, "It's obvious you've never been to the top."[3] Yes! Great achievements often demand great risks, but the exhilaration of the journey makes it all worthwhile. So, too, with the work of leading a passion driven congregation.

There is stress enough in everyday ministry, more than most laypeople would ever guess. There are, though, some special stresses, which grow out of the risks a staff leader must take if a church is to grow. One is the construction of a new building. Risk is always inherent in any decision to build, and yet for most congregations wishing to grow, the addition of more space is unavoidable. The important decision is what kind of space and how much. It's like shortening the legs of a table. Unless they are all equally shortened, the table won't work. Unless worship space, education space, programming space, and parking space are added in the right proportion, the results can be disappointing. And the person best equipped to decide this is the staff leader. During the year or two between first drawings and finished building, the pastor must press on with confidence. Clarence Randall, management guru, wrote, "The leader must know, must know that he knows, and must be able to make it absolutely clear to those about him that he knows." It is definitely scary sometimes to be standing up there at the very front. Unless, of course, you love it.

Another stress is that of changing one's own role as a church grows. The more a congregation achieves the reputation that goes with passionate ministry, the more a growing number of people find their ways to that church. Attendance continues to climb, and slowly, your role in the church and in the eyes of the members is changing. The intimacy of the past is now fading except for a few people to whom you remain close. In the face of this, keep one important consideration in mind. When new, perhaps young, people come to your church, they soon size things up and decide whether their generation can or cannot assume leadership roles. The chances are that most of your new young members will be limited to members of current church families unless new people see opportunities to become leaders as well. It is important to begin moving new members onto such groups as staff parish, trustees, long-range planning, adult education, and the other groups that determine the course of a congregation's journey. Painful though it will seem to a few, those longtime member saints who have always called the shots must accept the advent of a new leadership generation with the changes and new directions this may very well promise.

A third quality of an effective senior pastor is an understanding of collegial ministry. Earlier, large church management styles were top-down leadership. The staff leader pretty much ran things, usually with a coterie of leading lay members as counselors. Many older clergy still tend to favor this style. But the worldview of most younger clergy and other church professionals is different from those of former days. We have all heard horror stories by younger people who have served on a staff and become discouraged by a staff leader who overruled an idea one too many times.

The element that makes the collegial style of ministry different from the top-down style is twofold: it grants freedom to the other members to run risks without fear of criticism, and it allows them to know their leader as a human being. That can be a risk for the leader. Stephen Covey addressed this: "The most important ingredient we put into any relationship is not what we say or what we do, but what we are. And if our words and our actions come from superficial human relations techniques rather than from our own inner core, others will sense that duplicity. We simply won't be able to create and sustain the foundation necessary for effective interdependence."[4] There's the risk: letting your colleagues really know you. However, if you're a real friend, if you possess the character that your church deserves from their pastor, the warmth and comradeship that results will richly bless your life.

It should also be said that this only works if there is a high level of trust among staff members. An idea that doesn't work is not necessarily a bad idea. To work in an environment where one person decides what is a good idea and what is not will thwart everyone but that person. The current expression, "think outside the box" describes new ideas, untried, ground-breaking, and innovative. Isn't that what a church needs? The best way to encourage that kind of creativity is by letting people with ideas about which they are excited try them out. Of course there are limits, which anyone with good sense can realize, but the best venue in which to test that is the gathered staff. I wish I had kept a record of the number of ideas my staff colleagues conceived and carried out which I privately didn't think would work but later learned were great ideas. Finally, the day would come when I would be sitting in the chancel on Sunday morning scanning the back of the bulletin and read about some new program, about which no one had remembered to tell me. I loved it. I realized St. Luke's was not limited by the limits of my creativity. Instead, all our creativity went into the blender, and the results were constantly amazing. Each new venture served some need, reached some people not otherwise reached, and enabled the ministry of St. Luke's to relate God's love to more people. The effect of this was the arrival of new people in such numbers as to require the steady increase in staff size and lay involvement.

One example comes to mind. One of the ministers on our staff was counseling a young man who was struggling with grief over the death of his mother. Like a lot of men, he was bottling his grief inside, talking about it only with the minister. She conceived the idea of what she called a Grief Recovery Workshop. A meeting was announced, a limit was placed on the number of members so they could interact in the group, and when the program was announced, so many people signed up that it was necessary to conduct two workshops simultaneously. We'd had no idea so many people needed help working through their grief.

At the conclusion of one session two men were starting out the door. One whose baby had died was walking by the young man whose mother had died. One said to the other, "I guess we have to accept that this has happened and there's nothing we can do." The other turned to him, put his arm around his new friend and said, "There's one thing we can do; we can cry together." That was powerful stuff. In all the prior years of my ministry I had never thought of a program like that, but one young woman minister, more sensitive than I, had thought of it. I believe I first learned about the program while reading my bulletin one Sunday morning. It became a regular part of our church's life and touched—and still touches—many people.

It's worth reporting another occasion when I was walking down the hall past a fellow pastor's office and overheard her say to someone else something to the effect that "I have two camels and a donkey, but I don't know whether I'll have some sheep in time." I decided it was better if I did not know what was going on next, so I just walked on. A few days later I read that there was to be a live nativity scene, complete with Mary, her Baby, and a bunch of local angels, enacted in the churchyard on Christmas Eve. Sure enough, bleachers were erected, the scene was enacted twice, and interspersed between the two showings was an hour of hot chocolate and good conversation in the fellowship hall. Hundreds of parents, children, and single people attended; and this became an annual event at St. Luke's. I will assure the reader that I would never have thought of anything like that in a million years. Some of our programming ideas didn't work. That never bothered us. We'd give it a good try, and then, if people did not respond, we canceled that program and tried another.

Let's consider "burnout." The mistake many of us clergy make is the temptation to do it all, to spend energy and time on tasks others could do as well or better, and thus we have too little energy and time for what we do, or could do, best. I know pastors whose preaching is not nearly as good as it could be because they are so hyper-busy all week they don't spend the thoughtful hours reflecting, studying, reading, and as important as anything, sitting with friends and acquaintances listening to them tell about their lives. A preacher can only dispense what wisdom he or she has first obtained, and wisdom usually comes through a combination of a firm but informed faith, coupled with first-hand acquaintance of life's hard knocks and a growing understanding of the people whom one is called to serve. You probably have a copy of the poem about a pastor who resides in a tower, reading, praying, thinking, and finally in a time of mortal crisis he calls out to God, "Where are you?" and the reply comes back, "Down here, among my people."[5]

It has been popular of late for us ministers to complain of burnout. I would guess it results from repetitive performance of work one doesn't really like to do. If a church is to grow in a healthy way, one not dependent on some highly charismatic personality who will take the church's spirit when he or she leaves, it must be accomplished by a strong and rich variety of personalities which, when merged into a dedicated team can, together, move toward the goals they believe God has set for them. The staff leader is not to do it all. He or she is to empower many people, working together, to do it all. Many lay members of the congregation will be glad to share the burdens.

This brings up a dilemma faced by many clergy, one which contributes to burnout, and one of our own making in most cases: the imagined expectations of church members. Obviously certain expectations are legitimate. The role of a pastor is fairly well understood by most church members. What sometimes is not understood is the specifics, the behind-the-scenes stuff, things like long phone calls, district meetings, drop-by parishioners with problems, what Carroll Wise used to call "counseling on the hoof." Then there are staff meetings, letters to answer, visits to bereaved families in preparation for a funeral the next day, marriage counseling, speeches to the Lion's Club, professional journals to read, one-on-one discussions and brainstorm sessions with staff colleagues, not to mention the irreducible minimum of meetings of various sorts, most of them at night. If the pastor is also to study, pray, prepare sermons (really good preachers spend a lot of time at this), counsel troubled people, perform weddings and funerals, meet with people about baptism, spend time with other pastors cross-fertilizing ideas, fulfill some of the bishop's expectations at the district and conference level, read the latest good scholarly book—the lay reader gets the idea. The pastor, if he or she is going to have any kind of life as spouse, parent, family member—sometimes there just aren't enough hours in the day, nor energy units in the body and mind.

Since it's not possible to do it all, too many of today's clergy finally fall in the traces and suffer one or another malady having to do with guilt, anxiety, feelings of falling short, or hostile defensiveness.

Here's what I did many years ago. One night I assembled the staff-parish committee with some other key leaders, and using an easel and newsprint I asked them to list the various things they expected from a pastor. The list was two pages long. I then asked the members to put their minds in neutral so they didn't keep a private tabulation and to assign the amount of time they felt I should allot for each responsibility each week. When we were done, we added the list. It totaled eighty-six hours. Everyone was flabbergasted. I then asked them how many hours they felt it fair to ask their pastor to work. It was more like fifty. So I then requested that they begin paring the list, eliminating some things, reducing others.

Beware the Messiah complex, the feeling that we are somehow falling short of Jesus' expectations of us if we don't touch all the bases. I look back on my own several years as an active layman in my church, and I recall just what I and my friends did and did not expect from my pastor. What I did expect was that he preach his very best, that he be available to me in a time of crisis, that he maintain his studies, and that he be caring in seeing that very elderly or ill people felt looked after, loved, and valued. Maybe I should add that I expected him to be an admirable role model for me. I did not care a hoot what else he did with his time.

What about those people with whom we work, people not so able to control their own destinies as is the senior pastor? I have a small paperweight on my desk that bears this inscription: "If you are not the lead dog the view never changes." Behind that indelicate reminder is an important truth, one the wise staff leader never forgets. Life can get boring if you do the same old thing over and over. I am convinced the main reason good staff people leave is for this reason. Creative people want and need new fields to conquer, changing challenges. We at St. Luke's made sure that everyone had an annual opportunity to take a long view of one's own ministry in the context of the overall ministry of the church and to revise, redefine, get away from onerous tasks as they might seem to the individual, and take on new duties of their own choosing. Of course this becomes easier as a staff increases in number. However, in some degree this can and must be done in every staff situation, or the drones will tend to remain for safety's sake and the leaders will be out looking for a place to shine.

One important dimension in this process is the need for all program staff members to have areas of responsibility in which they are the lead dogs. The more responsibility you place on my shoulders, the more my pulse will race, my juices will flow, and the more fun I'll have showing you, the congregation, myself, and God what I can do. But remember one inviolable rule of management: *You must give authority equal to the amount of responsibility you assign.* One friend of mine who became one of Indianapolis's leading Methodist pastors told me of the time he was assigned as young co-pastor (a situation which rarely works) to an older, soon-to-retire pastor whom we'll call Dr. Jones. One evening, shortly after he had assumed his responsibilities, he met with a committee of leading laity and proposed a new program for something or other. The chair of the committee listened politely, then said to my friend, "Well, that sounds like a nice idea. Let me talk to Dr. Jones, and if he thinks it's OK, we'll try it." Right then my friend knew it was going to be uphill. With equal responsibility to Dr. Jones but, in the eyes of the church leaders, a lack of authority, he knew he would be unable to be effective. This applies equally to laity who accept leadership roles in our congregations.

Take periodic study leaves. I never met the slightest resistance to the idea from my laypeople as long as, upon my return, there was some evidence that the time away had made a difference. Find a place where you can be at peace, away from the phone, the clamor of duties left undone. Write your worries in the sand of life and let the tide wash them away. Banish guilt as you spend whatever time you must in your place of peace and happiness. Whatever your failures, your regrets, your disappointment, hand them over to God. Sit quietly. Leave only when you know you're ready. Go there as often as you must, and you will realize that you're not alone. Your parishioners will support you in this.

Here, I realize, is the ultimate antidote to burnout. Step away from the daily demands of ministry, go back where it all began, back in your mind, back in your heart, back to the place where certainty overwhelmed you and you knew what you must do.

Reflections on Chapter 2

M . K E N T   M I L L A R D

Carver has written about the qualities needed in a passionate, visionary, and effective local church pastor of a growing congregation. I would like to talk about how such a pastor can inspire laypersons to become passionate, visionary, and effective in their own ministries in a local congregation.

In his book *The Purpose Driven Church*, Rick Warren of the Saddleback Community Church in Orange County, California, says that most churches flounder because they do not have clarity about the purpose for which God has called them into being. When he started the Saddleback congregation in 1980, he knew that God had called him to start a congregation for unbelievers. He designed his ministry plan *with* people who had no previous church experience, and everything was planned *for* people who had no previous faith experience. They are so determined in reaching unchurched people that they do not like to receive members by transfer from other congregations because they are concerned it will deter them from their primary purpose.

Rick says: "We've never encouraged other believers to transfer their membership to our church; in fact, we have openly discouraged it. In every membership class we say, 'If you are coming to Saddleback from another church, you need to understand up front that this church was not designed for you. It is geared toward reaching the unchurched who do not attend anywhere."[6] Rick Warren has kept his congregation completely focused on its purpose, and it has apparently been very effective since about 17,000 people are now attending the Saddleback Community Church.

We believe that every congregation has been raised up by God for a purpose, and those churches that grow and flourish are those which have heard God's clear call for them and keep all efforts focused on their vision and mission.

However, while it is essential to keep our eyes focused on our purpose, we also need to have a passion for that purpose or it will never be achieved. A congregation with purpose but no passion has no energy to achieve the goal, and a congregation with passion but no clear sense of purpose has energy but no clear sense of direction and will feel scattered and unfocused.

Charles Powell, a management coach, makes a distinction between purpose and passion. He maintains that a person with a clear purpose says, "I will do this!" while a person with passion says, "I love to do this!" Purpose comes from the head while passion comes from the heart. He says: "A person of purpose will get it done regardless, but a person of passion will set everybody else on fire when he does it." He also quotes G. W. F. Hegel, who said: "Nothing great in the world has been accomplished without passion."[7] Ideally, a person or a congregation will have a clear sense of purpose as well as the passion or energy to move towards it.

A passion driven congregation is a congregation whose leaders model passion and enthusiasm for their ministries and who encourage all those in the congregation to discover the passion inside themselves, fan it into flame, and let it set the world on fire.

Before I preach I always pray a prayer attributed to the founder of Methodism, John Wesley. I pray: "O Lord, help us to become masters of ourselves that we might be the servants of others. Take our minds and think through them, take our lips and speak through them, and take our hearts and set them on fire." My desire is that the people would experience the living presence of God in worship so strongly that it would set their hearts on fire and rekindle the fire of God within them.

In Genesis 1:27 we are told that God created all of us in God's own image. There is a divine spark of God within each person, and Christian leaders are to affirm that spark within the lives of each person they seek to lead, nurture it, and fan it into a life energizing flame. Sometimes we refer to this spark as our eternal soul or the spirit of God within us. The image of fire is used to express the coming of the spirit with power at Pentecost when we're told that tongues "as of fire" appeared and filled each of the first disciples with the Holy Spirit.

When Jesus was asked by the Pharisees when the kingdom of God was coming, he told them that God is not coming with things that can be observed. Nor can you point to something outside of yourself and say "there it is" or "here it is." In fact, Jesus said, the kingdom of God is already here; it is "within you" (Luke 17:20-21). Now, I am aware that many contemporary translators translate the Greek word *entos* as "among you" rather than "within you." However, whenever the word *entos* is used anywhere else in the New Testament, it is translated as "within you," and it appears to be in harmony with Jesus' message in John's Gospel which says that God "abides" in us.

If we take seriously the idea that the image of God is a spark of God's spirit within each of us and that the kingdom of God abides within us, then the role of the church is to recognize, encourage, coach, and fuel that flame within each member of the congregation. This is what it means to be a permission giving and passion driven church, which not only gives permission for people to fulfill their own ministries but actively encourages it.

Several years ago a man in our congregation died in a plane crash, leaving behind his wife, a twenty-one-year-old son, and a thirteen-year-old daughter. At the funeral service we recognized our deep pain and loss, but we also thanked God for this man's life and all that he had meant to us, affirmed our belief in eternal life, recognized that death is not the end of life, and surrendered his eternal soul into the hands of our loving God. In the weeks that followed his death, we tried to help the family face their grief and loss and walk through it to discover God's light and hope on the other side. Brooke, the thirteen-year-old daughter, had a particularly hard time accepting her father's death and expressing her deep pain and loss. Pam, a therapist in our congregation, worked with Brooke for some time to help her express the anger and pain she felt over her father's death, and to then take the next steps in her life.

After helping Brooke through her grief and pain, Pam came to the conclusion that children and youth grieve differently from adults and need their own ways to work through the loss of a loved one. Pam read and studied a great deal about helping children and youth through the grief of a loss and developed a passion to minister to children and youth when they lose a loved one. Pam came to see me and told me of her passion and asked if the church could help provide a ministry for grieving children and youth. We said, "Of course." When God gives someone a passion for a particular ministry, we want to do all we can to help facilitate and encourage that ministry.

Pam enlisted many of her friends in her vision, established a board of directors, solicited funds from people throughout the community, and started Brooke's Place for helping grieving children and teenagers. The church provided the facilities for their meetings and today, five years later, there are 75-100 grieving children and youth from all over Indiana meeting every Thursday night, along with 20-25 counselors and volunteers who are trained to help children and youth work through their grief in their own individual ways.

One Thursday night I joined the Brooke's Place meeting for pizza before their evening small support group meetings. A little girl about nine years old came up to me and shared a booklet she had written and illustrated. She went through page by page telling me about a little girl who was sitting on the porch of her home when her mother came to her in tears telling her that her father had just been killed in a car accident. She had a picture of the little girl lying on her bed with a pillow over her head crying in disbelief. She also had a picture of a little girl going to school and fighting with other children when they teased her because she didn't have a daddy anymore. The next picture was of the little girl in the principal's office because of her fighting with other children. She told her principal about her dad's death, and the principal came and hugged her and told her that she also had lost her dad when she was a little girl and knew how the little girl felt. On the final page of the booklet there is a picture of a little girl smiling and the words, "Now the principal is my friend."

Experiences like this make me realize how important it is to encourage and support the passion of others because this is one of the primary ways God is seeking to care for and lead people today. At St. Luke's our Singles Ministry, Deaf Ministry, Satellite Ministry, Television Ministry, African-American Church partnerships, orchestra, work projects, pre-school and kindergarten ministries, music outreach ministries, spiritual life ministries, healing ministries, and all the other ministries of the congregation have arisen out of someone's God-given passion which the leaders of the church encourage and nurture.

Sometimes when a layperson develops a passion for a new ministry, the church has so many committees and procedures to follow before it can be approved that the person becomes discouraged and feels like his or her spark for ministry is being dampened rather than fueled by the leaders of the congregation. Many church committees seem to be designed to prevent ministry from happening or to raise so many doubts and fears that the person proposing it is discouraged from the get-go. However, we have instituted a policy that our goal is to encourage and facilitate ministries initiated by laypersons as well as staff rather than to discourage them. Rather than talking it to death at a committee meeting, we encourage people to try it, and life itself will tell us in time if it will work or not. We have had some glorious failures. But if you don't take the risk of failure, you'll never have great success.

If anyone brings a new ministry to us that is in harmony with our vision of transforming the world around us and our mission of sharing God's love with all creation, then we do all we can to help that ministry come to fruition. We also have a policy that lack of funds cannot be a reason for preventing a ministry from proceeding. Many times people will say that a certain ministry is a good idea but that we can't do it because we don't have the money. We believe that if God calls a person to a passion driven ministry, God will also provide the funds necessary for that ministry to succeed. Furthermore, we have discovered that in case after case, when someone follows his or her passion and church leaders support it, miracles happen, and funds become available from a wide variety of sources to provide for that ministry.

Sometimes, however, a layperson will come up with a passion or an idea for ministry, and they then want the staff or church leaders to implement it. This is the primary reason why many pastors and staff leaders don't want new ideas, because it could add more work to their already overloaded schedules. We believe that if God has placed the idea or passion within a person, then that person will have the God-given power to energize, develop, and fulfill that ministry. The lay leaders and staff can provide encouragement and coaching, but the time and energy required to fulfill that ministry will come from the person with the passion.

People often ask me how I keep all the ministries that are happening at St. Luke's under control. I don't try to control them. Like Carver, I often find out about them when I read the bulletin or the newsletter. My job is not to control the congregation; indeed, it is quite the opposite. My job is to surrender control of the congregation into the hands of God and to trust the spirit of God within each person to initiate and lead the ministries of the church. My primary responsibilities are to articulate through preaching and teaching the vision God has given this congregation and to pray for the people of this congregation and the world.

Sometimes pastors and staff are concerned that if they surrender control, then a dominating layperson will take over and lead the church in unhelpful ways. The point is that all of us—pastors, staff, and lay leaders—are to surrender ourselves into the hands of God and listen to the voice of God and not the ego desires of pastors, staff, or laity. My image is that we really are to be led by our God-given vision and mission. Whenever we are faced with a decision in one of our administrative committee meetings, I always ask, "How do you think a congregation which seeks to transform society would make this decision?" or "What do you think an open community of Christians who want to share God's love with all creation would do about this?" I am not the leader of the church; God's vision and mission for this congregation is our leader, and my role is simply to continue to remind us of our vision and mission and encourage us to be faithful to them.

People often ask, "How do you help people find their passion?" First of all, the pastors and staff leaders have to model it by identifying and living out of *their* passions. When the people in a congregation see a pastor, staff, and lay leaders on fire and excited about the passions for ministry God has placed within them, laity will begin to ask about the passion for ministry God has placed in their own hearts. One of our big problems today is that we often have dispassionate, negative, or cynical pastoral and staff leaders who wonder why there is not more passion and enthusiasm in their congregations for the ministries of the church. I encourage pastors and other church leaders to renew the vision and passion which first brought them into ministry if they want to inspire and lead others into renewed excitement and enthusiasm for ministry.

My wife and I adopted our interracial African American daughter, Koretta, when she was just one week old. Today she is married and the mother of three children and a social worker for the state department of family and child services. Being a biracial family has made us very much aware of the continuing effects of racism and white privilege in our society and has created in me a passion for interracial ministries to break down the racial barriers that hold us apart and to build bridges of racial understanding and communication. Because of my passion and commitment to interracial ministries, today dozens of our members are involved in inner-city tutoring programs in predominately African American schools; partnership ministries with three different African American congregations; biannual interdenominational, and interracial worship celebrations; racial study circles; and work camp projects in interracial communities in this country and beyond.

However, some pastors and church leaders seem to want everyone to be enrolled in their particular passion for ministry rather than simply seeing it as a model for others to discover and develop their own passions for ministry. Leaders need to model passion in ministry not so that everyone will be enrolled in their passion (though some will) but in order to encourage and facilitate others in finding their God-given passion. Fortunately, God has placed different passions for ministry in the hearts of all of us so that together we can be the whole body of Christ as Paul says in 1 Corinthians 12:4-7: "Now there are varieties of gifts, but the same Spirit; and there are varieties of services, but the same Lord....To each is given the manifestation of the Spirit [passion!] for the common good."

A second process we use to help people discover their passion is to encourage them to ask themselves the question: *What excites me?* When people look deep inside themselves they will usually find something that excites them about life or something that they find great joy in doing. I once knew a man whose passion was fishing, and he asked me how that could be used in ministry. In working with our singles group he discovered that many single moms had children who had never been fishing in their lives, and he thought it was terrible for a child not to experience the joy of catching a fish. Consequently, he announced a day when he and some of his fishing buddies would take any children fishing for free who wanted to come. About eighty children and their moms showed up, and it was a touching scene to see some of these old fishermen helping children to bait hooks and share in their excitement of catching a fish for the first time. Many moms thanked us for this program because their children usually didn't have many opportunities for positive relationship with father-figure and grandfather- figure type men. I learned that even a passion for fishing could be used by God for ministry to children.

A third question we ask people to consider is *What upsets me?* Sometimes what upsets us is simply the other side of the coin from what excites us. I once had a parishioner who was always very upset because the pastor didn't spend more time calling on the sick and shut-ins in the congregation even though she herself was not sick or shut-in. One day I was going calling on one of our shut-in members and invited this woman to come with me. In the course of the conversation with this member, we discovered she had arthritis and had a hard time getting out for her doctors' appointments and shopping for groceries. I asked the woman who was visiting with me if she would be willing to stop by each week and take our friend to her appointments and shopping, and she agreed to do so. They developed a wonderful relationship, and whenever I discovered another sick person or one who needed some regular pastoral care, I would call my formerly disgruntled friend to visit them regularly. She became our volunteer parish visitor. I also noticed that she recovered a sense of excitement and joy in her life because she had discovered her passion for ministry. It all began when she articulated what upset her in life.

We believe that God has placed a passion for ministry in the heart and soul of every person and that the role of the church is to help people discover that passion, encourage it, and fan it into flame. We believe God will use that flame not only to bring fulfillment to the person but also to transform of our world.

CHAPTER 3

SUCCESSFUL TEAM BUILDING

E. CARVER McGRIFF

My life prior to entering the Methodist ministry was good news and bad news as far as my life *in* ministry was concerned. The bad news was that I was ten years late arriving. Following two years in the armed forces, I graduated from Butler University with only a hazy idea of what I wanted to do for a living. In the next several years I was a salesman, then moved to Bloomington, Indiana, first as a manager for a small department store, then for the final four years, as owner of my own store. None of these was bringing happiness, much less success. In fact, it wasn't until one dark night as I was driving aimlessly around Bloomington, crying helplessly, pounding the steering wheel in frustration, and shouting at God in a most disrespectful manner, that God finally let me in on the secret. I was to become a minister, and nothing I did was going to get me out of it.

We sold our house, sending my parents into a tizzy wondering what would ever become of their eldest son, and spent a month at a lake while I read everything in sight. Then we were off to Garrett Theological Seminary where I was deliriously happy despite serving two small churches three days a week and doing graduate work four days a week.

One benefit from all this, the good news, was that some insights from the business world stood me in good stead in the church. For instance, I spent a year working for an aluminum company out of Chicago. I was their district manager, one of those jobs where you get a title in lieu of a good salary. I was assigned to a large grocery chain in Indianapolis and had a small desk near some of the executives. My job was to call on some fifty stores in the chain throughout the state of Indiana, seeing to the sale of my company's products. The two largest stores were in Indianapolis, one on West Sixteenth Street, the other on Southeastern Avenue. They were about equal in size and volume, and of course, the managers were competing for the top spot.

When I would stop at the store on Southeastern Avenue, I would always find the manager sweat-stained, clad in a filthy canvas apron, tearing open boxes, perspiration on his forehead, calling out instructions to several helpers. He was always civil to me but much too busy to get acquainted. I would do my work, then leave. Then I would visit the store on West Sixteenth Street. I even remember the manager's name. He was usually sitting in a chair in a small glass-enclosed office in the middle of the store, feet on the desk, chatting with some office employee. When he would see me he would sometimes say, "Hi, Carver, let's go get a cup of coffee." His hair was neatly combed, his tie straight, his shirt immaculate. He never seemed in a hurry.

One day I overheard a conversation in the main office to the effect that one of these two store managers was to be promoted to district manager. The Sixteenth Street manager received the promotion. The lesson was not lost on me. This manager knew how to delegate and how to choose the right people, then trust them. The other fellow was no doubt of the I-won't-ask-them-to-do-anything-I-won't-do school of management. While the other manager was at his very limit, the Sixteenth Street manager could handle a lot more. This didn't mean he was a slacker. He worked hard enough, but at the things he did best. His strength was *motivating* others and *empowering* others to do *their* best. I never forgot that lesson. Learn to select people wisely, delegate, and trust them if you want to grow.

Before listing my rules for building an excellent staff, let me offer a few comments. A church that waits until the congregation's size and budget permit the hiring of an additional program person will probably never hire one. *The church that will grow is the one with the vision to see an unrealized potential and is willing to run the risk of finding someone to bring that potential into reality.* In the course of my twenty-six years at St. Luke's our staff grew from two ordained clergy and one part-time education director, to six full-time and one part-time ordained clergy, and three full-time and one part-time education professionals. We also added a full-time youth director. And my point is this: *Each of those new people was placed on staff at a time when they weren't really needed based on the current size of the congregation.* And each time, the congregation grew.

Let me share one experience from the St. Luke's story. One day some of us were talking about the large number of single people in the surrounding community and the fact that, historically, churches tend to have "family night dinners" and "couples clubs" which exclude those single people by definition. So one evening a meeting was held to which only single people were invited. Five or six showed up, and the meeting was convened by a woman, recently married, but single for the six years prior to her recent marriage. Together that group decided to start a single's program, and they immediately scheduled a first meeting for a forthcoming Wednesday night.

We soon realized a professional staff member with singles as his or her primary responsibility would be needed. We went to the nearby Christian Theological Seminary and found a charming, single, second-year student pastor, a Disciples of Christ church member, who was interested in the position. With some reservations but with a sense of God's leading us, the finance committee and the staff-parish committee agreed to hire this young man to build a program for single people.

To jump now to the conclusion, pretty soon a hundred people were showing up for the Wednesday meetings. After two years the young pastor graduated and this time we sought, and found, a very talented full time pastor, and attendance passed 200, then 300, people per meeting. The day came when I received a call from a newspaper reporter in Los Angeles asking about our single's program, which was known two thousand miles away.

Now, for your finance committee, let me share this. One evening I was the speaker at the single's Wednesday night meeting. Rather self-righteously I later realized, I welcomed them all to the congregation, invited them to join us for worship if they wished (they had a worship service each Wednesday which many attended), then made the error of saying that we realized that many of them were on tight budgets and we would understand if they—I can't recall my exact words, but the import was—"won't be able to carry your own weight here."

The following Sunday, a young woman greeted me following worship, smiled, and said, "So, you think we single people can't carry our financial weight?" and handed me a check for two thousand dollars. We soon learned that many of them would become generous and regular members of the congregation. Of course there was a lot of turnover, but in the years that followed, some fifty to sixty weddings resulted from the singles meetings taking place at the church, and that included both of those pastors who found their beloveds. A surprising number of people moved from the singles program into leadership positions in the church. Today many of St. Luke's finest leaders began their life there as part of that group.

Here, then, are the rules I followed in building a large and effective staff. I have in mind paid staff, but these rules apply equally when working with volunteers.

The first rule is never criticize. Try to find something to praise.

A popular book of the 1930s and 1940s, *How to Win Friends and Influence People* by Dale Carnegie, reports the story of Charles Schwab, president of Carnegie Steel Corporation, the first industrialist to be paid a million dollars a year. That may be pocket change to the average CEO today, but at that time lunch cost a quarter and working people made fifteen dollars a week. So a news reporter interviewed Schwab and asked him how he could be worth that much. His reply was insightful, something any manager today should heed. He said he was worth the million because he knew how to motivate people to do their very best work. His most important rule was this: he never—that's *never*—criticized anyone.

Schwab was quoted this way: "*In my wide association in life, meeting with many and great [people] in various parts of the world, I have yet to find the [person], however great or exalted his station, who did not do better work and put forth greater effort under a spirit of approval than he would ever do under a spirit of criticism.*"[1] Schwab only praised. He explained that no matter how gently it is expressed, criticism inevitably drags a person down, whereas praise, offered honestly, inevitably causes anyone to work harder and do better. The few times I did criticize someone the consequences were always as Schwab predicted. I still have an unhappy memory of the time I criticized a colleague pastor in the presence of our staff. I was inwardly angry, and it probably showed. I later apologized. But apologies are often like trying to glue the pieces of a broken mirror back together. Many years later the man, a dear friend to this day, reminded me of that criticism and the fact that it hurt him deeply. It was a terrible mistake, one I tried never to make again.

Sometimes this isn't an easy rule to follow. However, I have only to turn the equation around, recall what I feel when someone criticizes me, to realize how nearly useless criticism is. If there are any exceptions, it can only be when the other person invites it. Even then some form of praise will be more effective. I'm obviously not recommending flattery or false praise. People who resort to that usually lose their effectiveness as others realize the technique. Then praise loses its value. But I know this: when someone sincerely praises something I do, it energizes me, makes me want to deserve and continue to deserve that praise, and in the process, I grow and raise my own sights. So, too, the people with whom I work.

The second rule is to seek self-starters who will take initiative with a new idea.

I decided the other kind of person would require too much of my time and energy for the relationship to be worthwhile. This doesn't mean I wasn't available to help if a colleague needed me, but what I really sought was people who had their own ideas and who were not afraid to fail if the idea seemed good. What I did not want was an assistant. A recent issue of *The Wall Street Journal* described the management style of Steve Case, chairman of AOL. His number-one motto was listed this way: "Hire terrific people, point them generally in the right direction and let them go." That's my idea as well.

One of the watchwords of our staff was "We encourage failure." Of course we didn't want to fail. But neither was there any reason to be embarrassed if an idea that seemed like a good one turned out not to work. The effect of this was that we slowly built a team of people with minds of their own, people who could be counted on to create new ideas and new programs, and who had the initiative to carry them out without fear of repercussions if their ideas didn't work. I didn't want people who would do my bidding. I wanted people who had gifts I don't have. That way the total of staff capability was dramatically increased.

I have seen churches with highly talented senior pastors who required their colleagues to pass everything by them for approval, who even sometimes said to wait until certain influential church members could be consulted. That thwarts initiative. Clergy who have served on such staffs invariably report that they finally reach the point of thinking, "What's the use?" and fall back into doing what they're told. If they are very talented and motivated, they start looking for another church.

The third rule is to try to see that each staff member has a happy life.

Obviously we wanted people who weren't afraid to work, but I also knew they must have time for family, time for leisure activities, and time for personal growth activities. I know senior pastors who get nervous if they don't see each staff member there in the morning and there in the evening. I learned that if I trusted my staff members and they knew I trusted them, two things happened. One, they felt far better able to arrange their work lives to accord with their personal lives and responsibilities, which contributed to their happiness; and two, they honored that trust by doing their jobs and doing them well. So by feeling the freedom to have time for their private lives, staff members often stayed for long periods of time. I also understood that if a minister's spouse is unhappy, the minister won't be happy either, so the whole family was included in my concern.

One of the considerations to keep in mind is to make sure a deserving staff member is as well paid as possible. Even though we are not in the work of the church to make a lot of money, we do have the same material needs as do the rest of our members. The cost of paying someone well is almost always less than the cost of frequent turnover, especially since the pool of really talented people is not all that deep. But the church in which the senior pastor's salary seems always to rise comfortably while staff salaries lag is almost certain to have constant turnover, and that almost certainly precludes growth. We also kept in mind the Methodist system and knew that the more ministers are paid, the fewer appointments there are to attract them away.

Some of us are morning people, some are night people. I made allowances for that, and as long as we were all on deck at the times we were needed, I was always content to let staff members operate on their own schedule. The more freedom a staff member feels to come and go to get the job done, the more that person will experience the exhilaration of serving and accomplishing something significant. This point cannot be too strongly emphasized: *All staff members deserve to feel like winners in the work they do.*

Does this conjure up an image of a dozen people dashing here and there, doing their own thing? Maybe there's an element of that. But because of our strong bonds of loyalty, teamwork continually won out. Each clergy person built his or her own smaller congregation within the larger congregation, which meant that as the number of staff members increased, I felt less required to know every church member and minister to everyone myself. True, some pastors don't like that idea. But if a church is to grow very large there is no other way.

Of course, some positions require predictable hours. Office staff must be present on a predictable basis. Those who run the church school must be present when the school is in session. But most programming staff positions are highly flexible. I always looked at the outcome. If the various activities of the church were running effectively, if laypeople were involved in increasing numbers, and if the steady flow of feedback was enthusiastic, I let everyone run.

The fourth rule is that if staff members become not only colleagues but friends, they work much better.

There's an old truism that familiarity breeds contempt. I disagree. Familiarity breeds understanding. Our staff clergy spent many hours together in various situations—social, work, or a combination of those—in which we came to know each other. We entertained each other in our homes, met for lunch or dinner, and in most cases built friendships that still endure. From this I learned one great truth: If people like you, they will work for and with you and genuinely celebrate your success. If they sense that you like them, they will know that they can trust you for the same support.

Need I add that if they don't like you, there will be times when you're on your own? Besides, I decided life's too short to miss out on the joys of close and valued relationships with people I could admire and respect. We often had fun together, with inside jokes, shared social activities, genuine caring about each other so that if someone was in dire need, someone else was always quick to step in and help.

Was there conflict? Of course there was. There has to be room for disagreement, misunderstanding, and just plain irritability. But the closer our friendships became, the more important it was for each of us to see that the relationship was never damaged.

There is a complexity here. Christian psychotherapist Paul Tournier identifies it this way. "It is not possible for people to work together at a common task without there being differences of opinion, conflicts, jealousy, and bitterness. And in a religious organization they are less willing to bring these differences into the open. They feel quite sincerely that as Christians they ought to be showing a spirit of forgiveness, charity, and mutual support. The aggressiveness is repressed, taking the form of anxiety."[2]

It's true, some of these negative feelings are inevitable in large staff relationships. The only adequate antidote is prayer. But prayer can be used to manipulate, and it's the solemn task of the senior pastor to pray with the openness that affords her or him the wisdom and sensitivity to deal with the anxiety inherent in a working team's relationships. I feel, though, that the more a healthy, loving friendship occurs among the members, the more this anxiety is either disarmed or turned to a good. After all, it has been pointed out before that all worthy achievements are accomplished by people troubled by anxiety. If it motivates us to action it is, in God's hands, a force for good.

Also, a number-one complaint by some staff members of larger churches is lack of communication. The senior pastor is off on his or her own track, and frequently, staff members simply don't know what's expected, what's happening, and how they're doing. A staff member should feel completely free to tell the senior pastor if this is a problem. The more we are dealing with each other as friends as well as colleagues in ministry, the easier it is to keep open the pipelines of communication. This is really important in both directions.

In the early going, each St. Luke's staff member looked to me as the central figure on the staff. As we grew, members bonded with each other so that interconnected loyalties caused one or another person to withstand temporary discouragement or failure yet continue work because of those loyalties. Many of the current staff of St. Luke's church have served there for many years and are probably there for the rest of their professional lives. One associate pastor was on staff for sixteen years, another for fifteen, another for eleven, another for eight. One current associate pastor is in her eighteenth year. Two others served for four years. Several were finally moved by the bishop to fine senior pastorates elsewhere. Any effectiveness I had in my later ministry was due in great part to the love, the loyalty, and the talents of those people.

The fifth rule is to make sure the other staff members feel valued and welcome.

A recent article in *The Washington Post* described relationships in the workplace as being just like those in high school. "The cliques of youth can take shape on the job," wrote columnist Amy Joyce, referring to feelings of rejection and exclusion which often result from the sorting out of relationships where we work. She went on to point out analogies to the cool kids of high school, the soccer players for example, as compared to those she referred to as "nerds" or the members of the chess club, and suggested the same phenomenon takes place where people work in the adult years of life,[3] and this includes the church. Feelings of being left out are probably universal.

One long-time friend of mine, a Methodist pastor, once remarked to me that he hates attending annual conference. I asked him why, and he frankly explained that everyone—he was referring to other clergy—heads out for coffee or lunch or dinner or evening fellowship, and he senses that for him to invite himself along would be an unwanted intrusion. In fact, one of the first things we pastors do at the conference is align ourselves with an "in" group to ensure that we aren't left out during play times. A natural tendency to be sure, but one which sometimes inadvertently excludes those who are thereby left with feelings of rejection and loneliness.

The *Washington Post* article described one young woman "on the verge of tears" as she described her own feelings about what she called the "caustic atmosphere" surrounding a clique in her office. Once, when they placed their orders for lunch, to be eaten in a private little gathering, she voiced her order only to have the others stare at her with disapproval for a long moment, then ignore her for several days. "She now eats lunch at her desk" reports Ms. Joyce.

Exaggerated? Perhaps, or so we would like to think when it comes to our little fellowship at church. But don't be too sure. It's worth taking a little time to observe and think about this as the staff size increases. We clergy are usually on different schedules than the other staff members and easily fail to remain sensitive to those relationships. We're wise if we make sure this doesn't happen. The church where I currently worship has more than twenty staff members, and every Tuesday, following a full staff meeting, everyone goes to lunch. Everyone is invited, but if it appears some beg off, others make sure that it's the individual's true choice and not a private feeling of being unwelcome.

The primary reason for a staff leader to be sure on this point is sheer humanity. It's what Jesus would assume we would do. But also we do well to keep in mind the observation of Nancy Lynch, a professor of management at Medaille College in Buffalo, New York: "A sense of camaraderie makes people want to come to work each morning which reduces absenteeism and turnover.

People are much less likely to quit if they have friends at their workplace."[4]

The sixth rule is that credit and recognition for work well done must always go to the deserving staff member.

Psychologist William James said, "The deepest principle in human nature is the craving to be appreciated."[5] A wise staff leader takes this point very seriously. Don't sit at the head table if an associate arranged the event. Let that person be there. Be highly verbal in public about the accomplishments of other staff members. I learned one great principle a long time ago. *If you have a compliment to give, always do so when others are present.* If you feel you absolutely must deliver a criticism, be sure it is done in private. Giving strokes, if they're genuine, is a great investment in personal relationships. And certainly, as church members see the obvious warmth between their staff members, it tells them something about those people, which it is good for them to know.

One issue about which business people feel strongly is one with which I disagree: job descriptions. Of course some jobs require them. But here's what we did for many years. At the start of each church year the six clergy went on retreat for two or three days. On a newsprint easel we listed every responsibility we could think of that one or another person should perform. Whether it be to oversee adult education programming, or leading the youth, or running the athletic program—everything. It took us a long time, and we ended up with several pages of lists.

Then we asked ourselves, "Who wants to do what this coming year?" Time after time we realized that someone was getting burned out in a particular area, and often someone else wanted to take a shot at that. Presto, one person avoided burnout and another claimed a new area of ministry that was not assigned. It was an individual choice. Let me add something Bear Bryant, the famous football coach of Alabama, said when asked how he motivated his teams. He said he told them, "If anything goes bad, I did it. If anything goes semi-good, we did it. If anything goes real good, they did it."

Before long we had all redesigned our ministries for the next year. This, of course, is a luxury not available to smaller churches, but it attracted and held the kind of people needed at St. Luke's. I realized one important point. When a new member joins a staff, especially if that person is young and not yet very experienced, he may not know exactly what his true gifts may be. On a staff which holds rigidly to the original job description, that staff member may soon become unhappy, may outgrow the position and before long, will be looking elsewhere. On the other hand, given a situation where, as he learns new skills and discovers what ministries bring him personal joy, he can expand and, if necessary, eliminate, that staff member may grow into one of the most valued and effective persons on the staff.

The seventh rule is to seek people who are better at something than I am.

I learned early on that if the combined skill level of my staff was limited to my own skills, we wouldn't go far. At a few things I was very good. At others, I could get by. But at others, I was not very good. If a staff member was good at something at which I was not, then the total staff was enlarged accordingly. As each new clergy or program staff person joined us, the overall ministry of our church was enlarged. A wise senior pastor needs people who have different skills and talents if the overall talent pool of the staff is to increase and prosper. However, this brings up an indispensable quality of a senior pastor if a church is to grow: a secure personality. You and I know of pastors who are threatened when staff members receive plaudits for their accomplishments. Such commendation of others may feel like subtle put-downs to the supersensitive pastor. If that is a problem in the senior pastor's mind, it's not likely that church can grow. But the pastor who can feel, deep in the heart, a glow of gratitude and pleasure at seeing a staff member receiving accolades for work well done is well equipped to lead the staff and the congregation onward and upward.

Reflections on Chapter 3

M. Kent Millard

Carver has written eloquently about developing effective staff teams to help congregations grow. I would like to share some reflections on one of the biggest challenges in staff relationships: managing and resolving interpersonal conflict on the staff and between staff members and lay leaders.

I served as a United Methodist district superintendent for four years while I was a pastor in South Dakota. It was my responsibility to supervise sixty-five congregations and about sixty pastors scattered over one third of the state of South Dakota. I discovered that a district superintendent is primarily a personnel placement officer and conflict manager. I found that I spent most of my time recruiting pastors for churches, helping appoint pastors to congregations, and dealing with conflict between pastors on the same church staff as well as between pastors and staffs and some of the church lay leaders.

Since I found that I was so often called upon to manage conflict in local churches, I felt I should learn more about it and took a summer course on conflict management taught by Dr. Don Bossert at the Illiff School of Theology in Denver, Colorado. I learned one principle in conflict management that helped me immensely in my work as a superintendent and as the senior pastor of larger congregations. The principle is this: In situations of conflict, the presenting issue is never the real issue. The real issue is always the state of the relationship between those in conflict.

When pastors or laypersons would come to me expressing their conflict with each other, they would always begin by telling me what they believed the issue to be. Usually, each of them would articulate the issue quite differently, but I always kept in mind that whatever they said was only the presenting issue. It was the surface issue, and even if it were resolved, the conflict would continue with some other issue arising as the presenting issue. I discovered that the underlying, deeper issue in all situations of conflict is the state of the relationship between those in conflict, and if you want to resolve the conflict, you need to work on improving the state of the interpersonal relationships among all the persons involved.

When relationships between persons who work together are good, then they can work cooperatively through any differences of opinion about goals, processes, procedures, When the relationships are fractured, however, and people don't trust each other, it is almost impossible to resolve serious differences of opinion. Therefore, whenever there is a conflict between staff and lay leaders in the congregation, I seek to work on improving the relationships first and then we can resolve the conflicting issues among us.

When James and John asked for positions of honor beside Jesus in the coming Kingdom, their request stimulated a conflict between them and the other ten apostles. In Mark 10:35-45 we are told that the other apostles became very angry or furious with James and John, and with hot-tempered people like Peter upset I can imagine that a heated argument took place among them. So what did Jesus do? He called them to come together to listen to him (Mark 10:42). The first thing Jesus did was to bring them together; to sit them down next to each other where they had to encounter each other physically. When there is conflict, we want to separate from each other and distance ourselves from those with whom we disagree; but conflicts can only be resolved when we come close to each other and deal with each other as fellow human beings.

After Jesus brought them together, he recognized that they all wanted to be "great" or to be those who made a positive difference in the world. Then he told them this truth about life: "Whoever wishes to become great among you must be your servant, and whoever wishes to be first among you must be slave of all." Jesus explained that he himself did not come to be served but to serve and to give his life for others (Mark 10:43-45). In resolving this conflict, Jesus brought them together, recognized their common desire to make a difference, and then shared with them the truth that greatness does not come in dominating others but in offering yourself in loving service to them.

I have worked on a church staff both as an associate pastor and as a senior pastor, and I have discovered that conflicts and differences of opinion often arise whenever people, even Christian leaders of good will, work together. Whenever conflicts arise on a church staff, we should seek to follow Jesus' example of bringing people together, working to improve relationships among them, and reminding them that we are not an ego-driven organization but one committed to serving each other and the needs of others in the name of Jesus Christ.

When I arrived at St. Luke's it was clear to everyone that the clergy team had a great fellowship among themselves, as Carver has shared, and the clergy were inspired to follow their passions and dreams in developing the ministries of the church. Many long-term effective ministries of the church, like our large singles ministry, were developed because a pastor had a passion for that ministry. It became clear that the next step, however, was to encourage lay staff and lay leaders to follow the example of their clergy and develop ministries out of their own passions and dreams.

In order for lay staff and lay leaders to have more of a voice in the leadership and direction of the church, we have brought onto our staff more lay members of the congregation who have the passion and gifts needed for specific ministries. For example, a successful businessman in our congregation volunteered to become a key leader in our capital funds drive to build new facilities. He was very effective in inspiring confidence, organizing fund-raising activities, sending letters, and asking for commitments to the capital campaign. After our first campaign was over, we asked him to come on our staff as director of development, and he now oversees all financial, building, and business issues in the congregation and has helped us to raise over fourteen million dollars in our capital expansion program as well as increase our annual giving by about 12 percent each year. He sold his business and came to work for the church at a fraction of what he had made before because of his love and commitment to St. Luke's and his desire to help the congregation fulfill its vision. Furthermore, he has used his business skills to open The Oasis, a church bookstore and gift shop that gives people an opportunity to purchase inspiring books and religious gifts at church. This also generates additional income for the ministries of the congregation. His business acumen has helped us purchase additional property for parking and has led us through the processes of rezoning to remove church-owned houses in order to provide additional parking spaces for our growing congregation. He also has a passion for directing our orchestra and directing musical performances. He directed *Jesus Christ, Superstar* in our church sanctuary during Lent, which not only helped thousands of people experience the last week of Jesus' life on earth but also generated thousands of dollars to support other ministries of the church.

Another layperson on our staff began as a church school teacher and leader, was trained as a Stephen minister, and is now on staff full time as director of our Caring Ministries program. She has a passion for caring for people, and under her leadership more than one hundred twenty people have become trained as Stephen ministers and are providing one-on-one friendship ministries to persons who have lost a loved one, are facing a life-threatening illness, or face emotional distress, or are hospitalized.

Another member lost her husband, daughter, and father-in-law in a boating accident years ago and out of her deep experience of grief and recovery has a passion to help others through their times of grief. She has come on staff as my administrative assistant and director of our Grief and Prayer Ministries and conducts grief workshops to help people through the loss of a loved one. We have discovered that many people find their passion and their ministry out of their own painful experiences of life.

Numerous other laypersons who began as volunteers in a ministry related to their passion now find fulfillment in working full-time on our staff in those areas. One of the challenges in staffing congregations is finding effective, committed people who will make long-term commitments to a particular congregation. One of the best places to look for new staff is in your own congregation. This approach allows you the opportunity to work with people as volunteers before they are employed by the congregation. Today we have fewer full-time clergy on the staff than ten years ago because we have used those staff funds to employ dedicated and talented laypersons. We believe that commitment to the congregation's vision and long-term effectiveness have increased as a result. Truthfully, many pastors become associate pastors in large congregations to enhance their professional ministry career. Shortly after they have gained more experience, they move on. However, laypersons may be more committed to the ministries of the congregation than to their own professional movement up the ministry ladder. If congregations want to grow in reaching new people, they need to have long-term talented and committed clergy and lay staff.

Along with the addition of lay staff, we have also increased salary, pension, and insurance benefits for our lay staff. Compared to lay staff in a church, the clergy often have far better salaries, pensions, and insurance benefits, and we felt this to be an injustice which we have sought to correct.

As the number of staff members has grown, we have found it necessary to restructure the way our staff works together. In the past we would all meet together for a couple of hours each week, but more and more we found that this was not the most effective use of our time together. Consequently, we organized ourselves into ministry teams, which meet weekly or biweekly to plan and coordinate specific ministries. We then meet monthly as the entire staff to gather for food, fellowship, and celebrations. We also have a weekly half-hour worship service for all of the staff, which helps to keep us focused on the spiritual dimensions of our work together, as well as giving us time for communicating important matters facing the congregation.

Our primary team for leading the congregation is the Development Team, which has the purpose of coordinating the development of all the ministries of the church. As senior pastor I serve as chair of the Development Team and am in charge of vision development; that is, to help our congregation fulfill our vision and mission. Another staff member is in charge of the

Growth Team, which oversees our large and growing children, youth, adult, singles, and spiritual life ministries. Our music minister coordinates all of our Music Ministries. A layperson on staff directs our Caring and Outreach Ministries. Another oversees our Financial and Building ministries, and another pastor helps to coordinate all of our worship services. The Development Team meets every week, and our lay leader and chairperson of the church council frequently meet with us to help us keep focused on God's vision and mission for our congregation.

Our clergy team meets weekly for the coordination of our pastoral services (preaching, weddings, funerals, communion) and those other ministries which clergy are specifically ordained to perform. Our Celebration Team also meets weekly to evaluate the previous week's worship services and then make plans for future worship experiences. We have discovered that dividing the staff into smaller ministry teams which meet regularly is more effective in involving more people in the decision-making for all of the ministries of the congregation.

Our satellite ministry, The Garden, has grown so large that we have developed a separate leadership team, which coordinates about a dozen ministry teams for this outreach ministry. The Garden leadership team and the St. Luke's leadership team meet annually for communication, assessment, and mutual support.

We have sought to empower our ministry teams so that decisions regarding a particular ministry are made at the front line of ministry by those who are involved in carrying out those decisions. We have also sought to streamline decision making so that the church can respond quickly to ministry needs in the congregation and the community.

We have also streamlined our church council so that there are no "at large" members on it. In order to be on the church council you need to be the chairperson or primary leader of one of the ministry groups in the congregation. In other words, only people who are actively involved in some ministry of the congregation are on the decision-making council of the church. Our experience from the past is that some people who were "at large" members of the council and not personally involved in leading any ministry consequently discouraged the development of new ministries. Furthermore, the church council meets only four times a year and therefore has to trust all of the ministry committees to carry out the ministries of the church on a weekly basis.

Since relationships are so important in developing healthy teams, I seek to take staff members and lay leaders out to lunch frequently where we can talk about how things are going personally and professionally in order to maintain healthy, growing relationships. My image is that the staff members and lay leaders are on the front line of ministry. My role as lead pastor is to support them by helping to provide the encouragement, funds, and personnel necessary for them to be effective in their ministries. Many senior pastors live with the image that the staff is there to serve them, but for me it is just the opposite. I am here to serve our teams—to encourage, to coach, to inspire, and to help fan into flame the spirit of God within each person with whom I work.

Working in a church is basically dealing daily with interpersonal relationships, and the more we can increase our listening skills, our leadership skills, and our relational skills, the more effectively we can work together to transform our society into a compassionate, inclusive, and Christlike community.

CHAPTER 4

SUNDAY AT ELEVEN, AND ALL THOSE OTHER SERVICES

E. CARVER MCGRIFF

Gather almost any group of Protestant church people together and ask them what factors cause them to choose a church, to feel good about their church, or to search for a church if they are recent newcomers, and you can be certain the first one they mention is preaching. That's the Protestant way.

A few years ago Warren Hartman of the General Board of Discipleship and Robert L. Wilson, professor of church and society at Duke University, collaborated on a study of large-membership churches. They reported that "the most frequently mentioned source of dissatisfaction is poor preaching." Senior pastors and others serving on the pastoral staff," they wrote, " seldom mention the negative effect poor preaching has on the life and ministry of a church. However lay persons are critical of poor or what they feel to be ineffective preaching." The two authors concluded that "This underscores the critical importance that lay persons from large membership churches attach to the preaching ministry of their church."[1]

Let it be clearly stated that preaching is an art to be cultivated by those who lead the congregation. Phillips Brooks, more famous for his statement that preaching is "truth through personality," also wrote that "whatever else you count yourself in the ministry, never lose this fundamental idea of yourself as a messenger."[2]

The larger the congregation, the greater the percentage of church members whose only contact with the church is on Sunday morning at worship. I'm not aware of any statistical studies on this, but it appears to me that by the time attendance reaches 700 or 800, this must be about half the worshiping congregation. Lyle Schaller has pointed out that "today most of the truly attractive Protestant congregations find their church shoppers have already visited two or three other congregations and have several others on their shopping list. The less attractive congregations are discovering they have relatively few church shoppers and 70 percent never return a second or third time."[3] It behooves us, then, to be sure that everything is as nearly excellent as it can be. Preaching, music, liturgy, and the overall ambiance of the worship setting will determine a congregation's future. Worship is the heart of the life of a church. Isn't it interesting, then, and I suppose in some ways exciting, that these days, no holds are barred when it comes to innovation in the conduct of worship?

Something new has happened in American church life in recent years: the advent of enormous nondenominational churches commanding unbelievable (to us United Methodist pastors) incomes with attendance in the many thousands per week. This is all to be applauded, of course. But it's exerting a powerful influence on mainline Protestant worship. I have attended four such churches in the past year and have observed the generating force behind much change taking place in the United Methodist church on the corner. Pastors are making pilgrimages to these centers of creative change and are returning armed with an array of, to them, exciting ideas as to how things can be done differently.

I like some of the innovations. A young generation is coming along who grew up with Walkmans clamped to their ears and with visions spinning in their heads from the hours watching music videos. If the church is to reach that younger generation— and, make no mistake, if we don't reach the young adults, what some pundits are calling the Emerging Adults (that's early twenties to early thirties) there won't be much of a United Methodist Church left to worry about in a few years. I have two daughters just into their twenties. Both are avid church members and devout Christians, and both girls and many of their friends are bored by traditional worship. Part of that is age, but my observation is that given today's fast moving entertainment pace and given the high sense of urgency about life which I observe in most young people today and adding in the multiplicity of technological tools available for worship, traditional liturgy and the relatively plodding pace of much traditional worship is destined for radical change. This, in fact, is already taking place. Jesus warned us long ago not to put new wine in old wineskins, which are brittle from age and likely to break.

Take so-called praise music. There was a time when it was said that Methodists learned their theology from their hymns. Praise music doesn't always seem to me to have much theology. Frankly, I find it irritating the way music leaders keep making me sing the same lyrics over and over with no way of knowing how long it's going to last. I recently attended one very large nondenominational church, and we sang for thirty minutes before anything else took place. I had two reactions. One, I wondered what my wife would say if I quietly slipped outside and hunted up a Methodist church. But two, I saw hundreds of young people, those very ones we need to reach, singing their hearts out. Reaction two outweighed reaction one in that moment. I let my mind drift from verse 5, which was the same as verse 1, and reflected on the fact that today's church must discover the true musical preferences of the younger generation and—not cater to them; that sounds cheap—but reach them with our music. I suspect that when a generation of classical church musicians retires, the next generation of professional church musicians will come with repertoires of the very music I have just described.

Recently I've been attending a church where I'm beginning to like the praise music. Today, when I attend a Methodist church, I personally enjoy a good old Charles Wesley hymn; but when we sing the new praise music, I still feel good if I look around and find a lot of young people present because I feel sure there is a correlation between the music and their presence. I'll admit something else too. I used to be politically correct and seek hymns that reflected the theme of the day regardless of their singability by nonmusical folks. Nowadays, I love it when we sing the songs I like and couldn't care less whether their theology applies specifically. My guess is that not one in a hundred worshipers knows or cares about such niceties.

Some hymns are embarrassing. Bishop John Spong, an Episcopalian, cites hymns like "Have Thine Own Way Lord" as "wimpish."[4] Not a few eyebrows have been raised at the line "Don we now our gay apparel," and I still recall watching certain teenagers smirking as they sang "Now I raise mine Ebenezer." And that line in one hymn, "Take my silver and my gold, not a mite would I withhold," sometimes sung during services designed to wrest more contributions from parishioners in times of budget shortfall, is worth some thought. Try having the organist stop right there and ask the congregation, "What did you just say?" I'm not intending to make fun of beloved hymns. I am, however, aware that the antiquated terminology in many hymns seems nonsensical to many a new Christian.

Many a church is experiencing dissension about music these days. Keep in mind that many of those new people we wish to win to the church have not become familiar with traditional church music and come, instead, familiar with the music they hear in their own world. Since the very earliest hymns were often written to tunes familiar to those who hung out in public houses, there's nothing wrong with matching today's new music to the styles of the time. Being a lover of good jazz myself, I was transfixed recently while attending Willow Creek Church when their jazz band opened with a number that knocked my socks off. It actually helped me get ready to worship.

Quality of presentation is crucial. You can put a twenty-nine-dollar Walkman on your ear and experience music that sounds like you're in a concert hall compared to the music we older people grew up hearing. Young people will have higher expectations regarding music in the church whether it's new or old. As a church grows, one necessary advance the wise pastor seeks is in the quality of the music. Bishop Gerald Kennedy once quoted a high school band director who said of his students, "Those kids love music: they eat music, they sleep music, they dream music—if only they could play music." That describes too many choirs.

The day came when we decided we needed a paid quartet. The finance committee balked at first, but when we brought in four splendid singers, the music became great as they lifted many good amateurs to a higher level. The singers remained as devout and otherwise active church members, and for the first time our music program equaled anything in our city. *There was a clear surge of membership growth in the year following the arrival of those singers.* There's a quantum leap to be made musically in growing churches at some point in their lives. That's one thing I noted in all the very large churches I attended. Their music may or may not have been my cup of tea, but the quality was excellent.

If you do all this, the need for diplomacy will then become apparent. Long-serving choir members with "not bad" voices will not always take kindly to the plan to add paid soloists. A move toward professionalism in the music department may create a few disgruntled choir members. For this reason it is important that among the qualities one should seek in paid musicians is good-spirited sensitivity to the faithful members who compose the choir. But I have also noticed that if the added singers play it right, it isn't long before the rest of the choir members begin to enjoy, maybe even be thrilled at, the rising level of their music. Many a "not bad" voice has become a "darn good" voice when singing alongside someone who is *really* good, and in due time all is forgiven and the whole town is talking about the music at your church.

Back to preaching. Styles are as individual as fingerprints. There are four excellent preachers within easy driving distance of my home. No two are anything alike. But the operative word is "excellent." Each of us is unique in personality even though the truth is universally true. So our job is to grapple strenuously with that truth then declare it with power.

Now every one of us fancies himself or herself as a pretty good speaker. May I suggest a way to prove that to yourself? Ask some trusted church members to take some tapes of your last three sermons (no fair choosing the three best from the last five years) and ask them to loan them to some friends who don't know you, possibly people who live in another community. Ask them to evaluate your sermons. Talk about making yourself vulnerable. A few years ago I did this. I won't tell you the results, but I will say it's the ultimate form of evaluation.

Each of us has a value system that grows out of some combination of childhood training, life experience, and genetically biased inclinations, along with our growing Bible-informed faith which is filtered through the rest. So we have a wide variety of convictions about the specifics of our Christian faith. The content of our preaching will no doubt be dictated by this value system. But I do counsel this: make sure your preaching is winsome. That's an old-fashioned word, and it means "cheerful, pleasant, causing joy." Now I know all about the prophets and all those latter-day fire and brimstone preachers. I recall during the stormy sixties hearing two young Methodist ministers boast about the number of members who had left their churches because of their "prophetic preaching." They were so proud of themselves. But most people today cannot be reached with the saving Word unless and until they are brought to listen to the word. Paul said, "Faith comes by hearing the word," so first we have to bring them in and keep them there. Preaching done in love will connect better than angry diatribes every time. Someone before my time said, "to love to preach is one thing—to love those to whom we preach is another." People can tell the difference.

An early-nineteenth-century poet, Sydney Smith, wrote that "preaching has become a by-word for long and dull conversation of any kind; and whoever wishes to imply, in any piece of writing, the absence of everything agreeable and inviting, calls it a sermon."[5] That must not be allowed to happen. Rudolf Bultman once said that the Christian faith is always one generation away from extinction. A lot rests on the shoulders of today's clergy. The greatest sin of all is to be boring. So, whatever else we do let us invest ourselves, mind, body, and faith, in the preparation of and the delivery of preaching at our best. If the preacher isn't putting this ahead of everything else, spending the many hours each week necessary for the preparation of an excellent sermon, that church will suffer and it probably will not grow.

Another form of innovation sweeping the nation is the use of video screens. They are here to stay, and just as with contemporary music, the wise pastor gently helps the congregation get used to it. If I were starting over, I would urge the installation of the largest screens I could afford and the most upscale, formidable technology available so these screens could be maximized in their use. They have a number of valuable in-house uses such as close-ups of a person speaking, announcements, and words to the music being sung (checking out the copyright stuff). One of the most effective uses I have seen is at a church in Indianapolis called The Garden. It's really an out-point of St. Luke's Church, founded and pastored by Dr. Linda McCoy. A worship preparation committee meets each week, and among its members is a woman who devotes many hours of her life to seeking brief scenes from movies that help to illustrate the next Sunday's sermon theme. The scene, no longer than two or three minutes, is shown prior to the sermon, establishing a tone for the message. It is tremendously effective, and being visual, it impacts a young generation of people raised on television and who are, therefore, visual people. I predict there will be a lot of this in tomorrow's church world.

The Garden also specializes in contemporary music (not all religious), using a band composed of guitars, drums, and all the other things that go with that. The venue is a dinner theatre,

McCoy is an excellent preacher, and the attendance maxes out the seating capacity every Sunday, numbering some 800 people in three services at present. One wonders how many people might attend if The Garden had more room. While this will probably never be mainstream worship, it does reach many people who are, for a variety of reasons, uncomfortable in a traditional church. This worship certainly underlines the point that there are many people thirsting for the Word who are attracted to nontraditional forms of worship. Progressive congregations might be wise to consider off-site worship venues for contemporary worship.

I have always been amazed at preachers who tell me they organize their worship services in a way which pleases their members without raising the question, "What about those people who visit a time or two and never return?" Take this business of pausing to ask everyone to greet the people around them. I still remember attending one church in which the pastor asked us all to stand and greet the people seated behind us. That creates quite a comical scene. We never did that sort of thing at St. Luke's, and it's my guess that most of your members wish you didn't either. At least I'd ask them. Since some people felt we should do this, I began to ask members of my new member classes how they felt about greeting other worshipers during the service. A large majority didn't like it. I suppose all the cheerleaders in the congregation like that sort of thing, but I'll wager that the majority of your members would prefer to dispense with the greeting business. If we're there to worship and if we have sincerely tried to prepare ourselves in advance for the worship experience, we do not want to be diverted by some artificial act of cordiality which interrupts our focus on worship. I'm sure in my own mind that the custom is a negative not a positive. In her delightful book *Traveling Mercies*, Anne Lamott spoke for many when she said of flying in an airplane: "My idea of everything going smoothly on an airplane is (a) that I not die in a slow motion fiery crash or get stabbed to death by terrorists and (b) that none of the other passengers try to talk to me."[6] Some people just aren't that gregarious, and for them all this business of greeting everyone is an unwanted intrusion.

Back to those people who attend once or twice and never return. Why did they not return? We can assume your regular attendees are content with things as they are. If your church is growing in a healthy way, perhaps all is well. But what about those "no shows"? They may have a lot of helpful feedback to give you if they are asked. Is there something about your worship service that does not attract them? Suppose you were to appoint a committee of proven diplomats who would get in touch with those visitors. If there are very many such people the replies could be most helpful.

Last week I attended a service at the local United Methodist church and sat behind a family with a small child. Granddad did everything he could to keep the wiggly two-year-old boy quiet, and the boy himself was a delightful little fellow. But Granddad didn't hear a word of the sermon, and Grandma sitting next to him was so busy keeping an eye on Granddad that she surely did not worship either. Mom? She mainly looked over and smiled at her wonderful son, and all in all, I wondered why they were there. The lady to their right also wondered that, judging from her constant irritated glances. The young woman in front also turned around three or four times with that "What are you *thinking* about?!" look on her face.

Small children do not belong in a worship service. It frustrates them. I'd guess that for every adult who attends church because Mom and Dad brought them as children, there's another out there who never attends church because of the colossal bore of sitting through services which meant nothing to them in their growing years. They belong in church, but how much happier a small child is in a room where physical activity is the order of the day, overseen by loving surrogate parent people who care for them, than in the restraint of a parent who persists in shushing them and restraining their perfectly natural impulse to be on the move. I had a very difficult time concentrating on the sermon last Sunday, as did many other people. In truth, it's rude to keep a small child in worship. The wise pastor sees to it that excellent facilities are available for the child and that young parents understand that one noisy kid can spoil worship for many people. The apocryphal preacher, often quoted, who is supposed to have said, "Any time I can't outtalk a noisy baby I'll quit preaching" deserves what he probably got—a tiny church. I hope this doesn't sound as though I don't like children. In fact I adore them. But I agree with the wise man who once said that "promises are like noisy children in church, they should be promptly carried out." Granted, we may offend someone by emphasizing this, but we'll please hundreds of others.

One thing I noticed in the growing churches I have visited is a limited amount of liturgy. In today's church, things must move more quickly than in the past. Some people, of course, prefer the formal ritual of traditional worship. There will no doubt continue to be churches which preserve these forms. But one concern here is how the decline in mainline worship can be turned around, how more people, with emphasis on the younger generations, can be brought back to the worship of God. The reality is that change is afoot. The heritage of the past, honored to be sure, cannot be allowed to obstruct the movement toward a much more fast-paced, contemporary orientation with its emphasis on the here and now. I don't pretend to know where it will all end, but clearly, change is happening, and the pastor who seeks to win many to the faith does well to act accordingly. But this is critical: it must be done with dignity and respect. Somehow, we must retain the grandeur, the majesty of God's sanctuary, and the called people assembled with the contemporary feel of a relevant faith in a troubled world.

It would probably be wise for larger churches to consider a service, possibly at a different time than Sunday morning, devoted to quiet, contemplative worship. Taizé, for example. There are certainly many people who will simply find themselves unable to worship in settings such as we are describing here. The churches that are making the greatest difference these days are the ones that offer an expanding variety of worship settings thus enabling a maximum number of us to find just the right place where we can commune and communicate with God. After all, there's no *right* way to worship, only "the right one for me." At present, St. Luke's offers ten worship opportunities weekly, and all six pastors preach weekly.

What about public prayers? They're usually too long. The story is told of the time Bishop E. L. Waldorf of the Methodist Church was invited to give the prayer at the opening of the Republican National Convention in Chicago. After he had gone on for quite some time, Heywood Broun, a then-famous journalist sitting in the press pit, after listening with growing amazement, was heard to exclaim, "My Gawd, it's a filibuster." That's what old Halford Luccock called "the vacuum school of oratory." I fear staff members who, occasionally feeling thwarted at not being able to preach as often as they'd like, find the prayer time an adequate alternative. If you ask around, you may discover that the silent prayer time is more valued by most worshipers than the pastoral prayer.

Many years ago Professor Henry Kolbe taught a class on public prayer at Garrett Seminary. Each of us had to write out our prayers, and we all received failing grades if Kolbe caught us telling God something he already knew. The point was to sensitize us to the question: To whom is your prayer addressed? Is it a carefully crafted statement to the congregation? We've all heard of one preacher who is said to have forgotten an announcement he had pledged to the president of his Woman's Society that he would make until he got to the back of the sanctuary at the conclusion of the service. So his benediction began like this: "O Lord, as we go from this place, help us to remember that the UMW meeting has been postponed until Tuesday...." I suppose since God knows everything in our minds we can't limit ourselves to just what God doesn't know, but we can purge ourselves of unnecessary information that we would not include in our own private prayers. It's OK to ask God to "bless this church" but let's not ask God to "bless our First United Methodist Church here in Indianapolis." When I hear a preacher pray "help us to remember..." I know I'm either about to receive an announcement or a bit of chiding about one of my several foibles.

In other words, keep pastoral prayers brief, let them catch the feelings of the listeners, gathering all the yearning hearts together, and keep in mind that God is already aware of the need to bless some twelve or fifteen people on your list who therefore need not necessarily be named from the pulpit. Prayer in worship has power when the persons praying truly feel themselves addressing God, truly know themselves to be the intercessor called on behalf of their people, and give voice to those deepest urgencies of the human heart. Insofar as the person praying is aware that people are listening, let it be in the spirit of communal openness to the God who simultaneously reads each human heart and surrounds each with the specific form of divine love best designed for that person's present need. It is not a time for the reading of an essay on religion phrased as a prayer.

What about the issue of entertainment as an element in worship? Most of us learned in seminary from our professors of worship that "entertainment" is a no-no in a worship service. What we must do, *à la* Søren Kierkegaard's well-known analogy to the theater, is steadfastly focus all our attention on doing what we do for God. That is a lofty virtue, and I, for one, espoused that belief for many years. Meanwhile, all those people attending worship, oblivious to such purist ideas, responded to the services as I believe is true in all our churches, on the basis of their aesthetic sensitivities, which is to say, whether they liked the music and whether they enjoyed the sermon. My generation of preachers publicly explained that it wasn't proper to tell a minister that one "enjoyed the sermon," while privately hoping to hear those words often. Bruce Larson once likened most of us preachers standing at the door following the sermon to a puppy dog waiting to be patted on the head.

Times have changed. While we are certainly in church to praise and otherwise serve God, I believe that an enlightened view of worship understands that there is and must be an entertainment value present if worship is to win people to the church and to the faith. A splendid choir anthem, an inspiring solo, or for that matter, a bouncy singing group on occasion, can be pleasing, entertaining, and also good preparation to hear an inspiring, faithful and, dare we say it, enjoyable sermon. I'm not talking about someone getting up with a string of catchy stories and funny jokes. This isn't the Lions Club. Now that I'm able to attend a variety of churches, I am grateful to hear music that entertains and a sermon I can enjoy. Political correctness notwithstanding, I will argue that while the primary focus of worship must be on the worth-ship of God and all that implies and that a certain overall air of reverence is in order, the wise pastor understands and implements the entertainment values of worship as a necessary element in an effective Sunday morning. As for applause, a nearly unanimous custom these days it would seem, perhaps I'm getting jaded, but I'm finally getting used to it. For several years I discouraged the practice. What if they applaud Mrs. Williams's solo this Sunday but not Mr. Johnson's solo next Sunday? How does that make him feel? But since it appears everyone's solo gets applause these days, we may as well reason that it is, after all, a form of response, it does add a bit of life to the service, and maybe God doesn't mind. Besides, the preacher who discourages the practice will sound like a stick-in-the-mud so, unless it seriously offends, I propose we allow it.

Dr. Ron Anderson is professor of worship at Christian Theological Seminary in Indianapolis. We recently discussed these issues. He doesn't like the word "entertainment" as applied to worship, but we did agree that if it is defined as meaning something similar to "enjoy," it can be useful. An accomplished organist, Anderson reminds us that the true church musician, instrumentalist or vocalist, is expressing a personal faith when performing, not just trying to please one's listeners. This was a reminder for me that we still are in worship to please God, not each other, and that important sentiment must be held in tension with the matter of our individual responses to the various elements in worship. A classical musician, Anderson does like some of the better praise music and feels that it will be an increasing component in Protestant worship, although not completely displacing the hymnal.

The true heart of worship is the meeting of God's Holy Spirit with our openness to receive that contact and to respond as God would have us do. For most of us the physical surroundings and the various trappings of worship have value only insofar as they facilitate this divine-human relationship and produce in me a spirit of praise and obedience. Richard Foster in his *Celebration of Discipline* writes, "Singing, praying, praising, all may lead to worship, but worship is more than any of them. Our spirit must be ignited by the divine fire. As a result, we need not be overly concerned with the question of a correct form for worship. The issue of high liturgy or low liturgy, this form or that form, is peripheral rather than central."[7]

The role of the worship leader is to facilitate this encounter of worshiper and God. Because of the rich variety of personality and intellectual types in a congregation, there is little that can touch all at the same time in the same way. There will be an inevitable sorting out as people search out worship settings which "speak to them" in such a way as to enable them to set aside for the time any worldly preoccupation so as to turn thoughts and feelings toward God. As Foster wrote, "Forms and rituals do not produce worship, nor does the formal disuse of forms and rituals. We can use all the techniques and methods, we can have the best possible liturgy, but we have not worshiped the Lord until Spirit touches spirit."[8]

We won't all like the same preacher, the same music, the same physical setting. Some people are contemplative and deeply moved by Taizé worship. A much larger body of worshipers prefers the large venue crowded with people singing and praising. Still others are most touched by the solemn formality of very traditional worship. Some, apparently, respond well to the fire-eating preacher with loosened tie and perspiring forehead. Some people love the small church with its half empty sanctuary and the homey informality of the worship form which is part worship, part community gathering. One has to believe that God accepts all of this and loves us each for our offering given from our hearts. To again quote Richard Foster, "nowhere does the New Testament prescribe a particular form for worship."[9]

What about the overall movement of a worship service? The people we most wish to reach, the teenagers and the "emerging adults" (aged 20-34), spend hundreds of hours a year watching movies and television. Special effects in today's movies are blindingly fast-moving as compared to those of the past. I recently watched one of the well-known four-star movies of the 1950s, and I could hardly believe how slow and ponderous the action seemed as compared to today's movies. Every preacher should take time to watch MTV (Music Television). This is not a commendation of the music or the visual effects, but if your teenagers are watching it, you need to know what it's like. The scenes shift constantly with frantic gyrations by the performers. Everything in the lives of most young people seems to move at high speed. In a subtle, subconscious way, this breeds an impatience in younger people. This must surely translate into an impatience with many worship services today.

It might be a good idea for us to spend some time with those young people. Ask them what they think about our worship. Does it inspire? Does it open for them a higher vision, a better way, a motive to love the world? They are the future of the church. They are the ones facing a terrorist-filled world, and they are the ones who, if our nation is to remain a wonderful place, will need the strong faith by which to maintain it that way. I see some splendid young people coming into the church. My own hopes are high for tomorrow. But I base that hope on the faith that churches like our own Methodist church, presently in a worrisome state of decline, will regain her sight and will more effectively act out her collective faith with a new way for a new day as Jesus leads us away from the past into an at once frightening, yet marvelously exciting, tomorrow. Let everything we do be done with excellence as our aim.

Reflections On Chapter 4

M. KENT MILLARD

One of the principal reasons St. Luke's grew during the ministry of Carver McGriff is because he is a superb, engaging, and stimulating preacher. Countless people have told me that they first came to St. Luke's because they had heard about Carver and wanted to come and hear him for themselves. Many of them came and stayed. Following a great preacher is a wonderful challenge for any pastor. After arriving at St. Luke's I realized that I needed to be more diligent in my preparation for preaching, to read more widely, and to become more focused on the message God was seeking to deliver through me on any particular Sunday. I started spending more time in the prayer and preparation I gave to sermons, and I believe I became a better preacher because of it. I also believe that every pastor can become a better preacher if he or she will focus more time and attention to the prayer and preparation needed for God-inspired preaching. I know how easy it is for pastors to become so involved in church administration, counseling, and leading the congregation that sermon preparation is a low priority, but I believe that we will not experience revitalized congregations until we have better preaching from the pulpits of our churches.

Matthew summarizes the ministry of Jesus by telling us that he came teaching, preaching, and healing. "Jesus went throughout Galilee, teaching in their synagogues, proclaiming the good news of the kingdom, and healing every disease and every sickness among the people" (Matthew 4:23). When Jesus walked on the earth, people came to him because when they were with him they experienced the living presence of God. When he taught in their places of worship they felt as if they were hearing direct teaching from God. When he preached the good news of God's unconditional love for all people, they felt unconditional love in that very moment. When he healed people of all kinds of diseases and illnesses, they experienced God's presence with power.

When people come to worship today, they long for a living, vital experience of the lively presence of God in the service. They don't come primarily to hear a history lesson on what our great God has done in the past or to have a music lesson on various types of Christian music or to read a historic liturgy which meant a great deal to those who first wrote it. Since we worship a living God, people who come to worship should experience a living God and not a story about a living God. Now we can use Bible reading, preaching, praying, liturgy, and music as means of experiencing God's living presence, but the goal is to experience God and God's guidance and direction for our lives and not just some nice historic things about God.

The danger of preparing sermons and leading worship week after week is that we will fall into a rut of simply doing the same thing, Sunday after Sunday, without passion and enthusiasm for what our God is doing now. A few years ago many people were wearing bracelets with the initials WWJD on them, which stood for the words "What would Jesus do?" The admirable idea was to get people to ask themselves what Jesus would do in the various situations they faced in life today. The problem with this approach is that it implies that Jesus is dead and gone but if he were alive today, what would he do in any particular situation. I believe that Jesus *is* alive today and the question is not "What would Jesus do?" (if he *were* alive) but "What is Jesus doing?" (since he *is* alive and active in the world today). The challenge for Christian leaders is to become so closely attuned to the living Christ that we see what he is doing in the world today, point it out, celebrate it, and let him enroll us and others in his mission.

Community worship, then, is the time when we all come together to praise God for what God is doing the in world today, to celebrate God's unconditional love and forgiveness for all, and to allow God to enroll us in God's contemporary great news movement. Unfortunately, many worship services are dull repetitions of the same thing week after week, without any passion or enthusiasm for what our living God is doing now.

Several years ago, I led a seminar at a theological seminary for about seventy pastors and seminarians on preaching. I suggested that before we prepared the sermon for Sunday, we needed to prepare the preacher. I maintained that the preacher is prepared by his or her own daily walk with God; that ultimately all we have to share is our own living experience with God through our study of Scripture, our prayer life, and our life experience. If we do not experience God as a living presence in our own lives, then how can we lead others to experience the living presence of God in worship and through preaching and how can we testify to what our living God is doing in our world?

Then I asked the participants in that seminar to share with each other in small groups their own pattern of personal devotion; their own ways of developing a relationship with God by spending personal and private time with God. I recognized that we do not all do it in the same way and we may not always be faithful to our personal prayer disciplines, but I asked them to share their intentions for developing a relationship with God in their personal lives. Then I joined one of the groups to participate in the discussion. When I got there they said they were finished; no one in the group had anything to share on the topic of personal devotions. I asked them to share their intentions in devotional life even if they were not faithful in fulfilling those intentions. They were silent. So I asked, "Do you ever pray?" One pastor answered, "Yes, I offer a pastoral prayer every Sunday in worship. I believe that it is very important for a pastor to lift up the concerns of the congregation and the world in prayer every week in worship." I responded that I was glad that he prayed in worship every week, but I asked, "Do you ever pray alone when you're not in front of the congregation?" Again, they were silent. Finally, one of the pastors said: "I used to pray every day. My wife and I would read the *Upper Room* daily devotional guide after breakfast and pray for all of our family and all the needs in the world. But after I went to seminary, I felt we had outgrown that sort of thing, and we don't pray together anymore."

When I brought the large group together again I discovered that about 60 percent of the participants felt they had so many other more important things to do in the church that they did not have time for personal prayer and for deepening their relationship with God. It became clear to me that one of the primary reasons that worship services and sermons are often so dull and lifeless is because the leaders of those services frequently do not have a vital, personal, and passionate relationship themselves with a living God. The truth about life is that we cannot share what we do not have.

I believe that the ultimate issue in the current worship wars is not whether the service is traditional or contemporary, or whether the music is classical or praise. The basic issue is whether or not the leaders are sharing a living and authentic relationship with God or whether they are just repeating a conversation they have had about God in the past. I have attended both traditional and contemporary worship services that were spirit-filled by the living presence of God, and I have attended both traditional and contemporary services that were lifeless.

Bishop Rueben Job once shared a personal pattern for devotional living, which I have found helpful both for my own spiritual journey and my leadership role as a spiritual leader in worship. Bishop Job said he gives one hour a day, one day a month, and one week a year in developing and maintaining a vital personal relationship with God. I have adopted his suggestion for my own life and seek to spend one hour each day in prayer, meditation, Scripture reading, and journaling, using as a guide the book *A Guide to Prayer for All God's People*, by Rueben Job and Norman Shawchuck. I also set aside one day each month for a personal spiritual retreat and attend a week-long spiritual retreat each year. I also visit with a spiritual friend each month to discuss John Wesley's question: "How is it with your soul?" While I have never kept these disciplines perfectly, it has been a strong enough pattern to help me be aware of my failures, experience God's forgiveness, and to help keep me focused on Christ and his will for my life. I am convinced that if every pastor and worship leader would focus more personal attention on spiritual disciplines and their relationship with God, life and vitality would return to the worship services we lead.

In addition to affirming what Carver has written about the need for excellence in preaching and music, I would encourage a deeper personal walk with God for all pastors and worship leaders who want their people to experience the power of the living God in Sunday morning worship.

I would also encourage pastors and church leaders to provide their people with some variety and alternatives in their worship diet. Not all of us like the same kind of physical food; some of us like Italian, some Chinese, and some traditional American food, and sometimes we like different types of food on different occasions. In a similar way, not everyone is nourished by the same type of spiritual food. Some people feel close to God in a highly liturgical Roman Catholic mass while others may experience the presence of God in a hands-raised-and-clapping charismatic worship service, while still others may find God in a more traditional Protestant worship service. I don't think God really cares one way or the other, as long as it is a service in which we experience something of God's power and love for us and surrender ourselves into God's hands.

At St. Luke's we have decided to offer a variety of types of worship experiences each week in order to reach as many people as possible with the good news of Jesus Christ.

As Paul writes in 1 Corinthians 9:22-23: "I have become all things to all people, that I might by all means save some. I do it all for the sake of the gospel, so that I may share in its blessings." Paul was willing to use many different means to reach the people of his day with the good news and, in a similar way, we need to be willing to use many different means of worship to reach the people of our time with God's good news.

St. Luke's currently offers ten different worship services each week, and we consider each of our pastors as a preaching pastor who has primary responsibility for one or more worship services. As the lead pastor, I have primary responsibility for three lively traditional services in our main sanctuary every Sunday morning. I meet each week with the Celebration Team, which includes all the staff members related to worship, where we evaluate the previous week's service, make plans for the next week's service and look at our long-range worship planning schedule. While we follow a similar pattern of worship each Sunday, we focus on how the quality of everything we do will bring glory to God and inspiration and hope to the congregation. Our Minister of Music has developed eighteen choirs, which have a total enrollment of more than 300 musicians. We are constantly told that the inspiration provided by a high-quality music program attracts many people. In our new sanctuary we have both a marvelous new pipe organ and video screens where we display all the words to the hymns, the creed, and often show pictures or videos to illustrate the message.

Dr. Linda McCoy, who has been on our church staff for over twenty years, has primary responsibility for four nontraditional worship services called "The Garden," which are held at two different satellite locations. A Disciples of Christ pastor who serves on our staff has primary responsibility for our Singles Service held at 12:30 each Sunday and our Later@StLuke's contemporary service held at 6:00 each Sunday evening. Our Teaching Pastor has primary responsibility for our Word on Wednesday (WOW) service, which is a Bible expository teaching service held at 7:00 on Wednesday nights. A layman who is deaf now leads our service for persons who are deaf and their families at 11:00 on Sunday mornings. In addition to these weekly services, we also have a monthly Taizé service of music, scripture, prayer, and meditation. Since bringing an African American pastor on staff, we will be starting a new spirit-filled interracial service at the church to minister to the interracial families in our congregation and to reach more persons who appreciate a more lively African American type of worship service.

As a passion driven congregation, we encourage the development of each of these services which grows out of the passion of a pastor and/or laypersons who experience God in these types of worship opportunities.

In developing the contemporary services at a dinner theatre, we discovered that necessity is still the mother of invention. In the early 1990s before we had built a larger sanctuary, we discovered that we were regularly overcrowded in worship and began to explore ways to have off-site worship services to relieve this problem. We approached members of our congregation who own a dinner theatre to explore the possibility of having nontraditional worship services there on Sunday mornings. They agreed to donate the space to us, and Dr. Linda McCoy began to work with one of the co-owners of the dinner theatre and a wonderful musician in developing this new satellite service. In the meantime, Linda had had an epiphany experience in which she heard the voice of God telling her that she would develop a new ministry. This vision gave her the passion and motivation to do all of the hard work necessary to develop and lead a new worship service. Linda and the co-owner traveled all around the country visiting other contemporary worship experiences to gather as much data as possible about starting a new service. They discovered that most of the large, growing, contemporary service congregations were very progressive in method in terms of using video clips, contemporary music, and drama but were very conservative in their theology. They proposed that we start a nontraditional service at the dinner theatre which would be progressive both in method and in theology. We enrolled about sixty people from St. Luke's to be the pioneers in developing this new service called "The Garden," which would seek to attract unchurched, dechurched, and antichurch persons, as well as those who simply prefer contemporary worship experiences.

We shared our vision with our regional denominational officials, and they helped start this new satellite service by providing funds for publicity and staffing. The first service was held in September 1995. After seven years we now have more than 800 people worshiping at the dinner theatre in three worship services and more than 250 people worshiping at the banquet hall in one service each Sunday morning. About 70 percent of those worshiping at one of The Garden satellite services tell us that prior to coming to The Garden, they had never attended worship at all.

A man who was in treatment for drug addition began to attend The Garden and heard one of Linda's sermons about how God offers forgiveness and a new start to everyone no matter how badly they have messed up their lives. He had lost his wife and family, his job and his home as a result of his drug addition, and felt there was no hope for him. But at The Garden, he experienced the living presence of God, loving him and forgiving him, and it transformed his life. He became drug-free, got a new job, and is now a regular volunteer at The Garden and maintains that the service at The Garden saved his life.

A woman who had left an abusive relationship with her ex-husband came to the service feeling lost and hopeless. She experienced the love of God filling her full to overflowing, and she felt called to a ministry with other women who had been through abusive relationships. She explained that she went back to her abusive husband three times because when she had to leave the abuse shelter, she had nowhere else to go. Consequently, she started a group called Fresh Start, which provides emergency funds, furniture, and counseling for women who want to set up their own apartment and begin a new life rather than return to their abuser. She, too, would say that this nontraditional, contemporary satellite service from St. Luke's saved her life.

Another person at St. Luke's had a passion to establish a ministry for persons who are deaf, and today we have a deaf ministry that provides a signed worship service, Sunday school, and fellowship opportunities for deaf persons and their families.

The Reverend Carolyn Scanlan is a single pastor who helped develop and now leads a service for singles each Sunday at 12:30 P.M. I call it an intensive care service because most of the single persons who attend have recently been through divorce and often feel unaccepted at their former church or find it painful to worship in a traditional service with many couples sitting together. They need a time to heal and to experience God's unconditional love for them, and the singles service is designed to provide this kind of experience. For some single persons, this service becomes their home church community. Others float among our other worship services. Many make a decision to eventually unite with the congregation.

We discovered that many people work on Sunday mornings and therefore cannot attend Sunday morning worship services. Consequently, the Reverend Scanlan developed a Sunday evening contemporary worship service called Later@StLuke's, called together a delightful singing group called the Later

Singers, and now about 150 people identify the Later service as their service of preference. Once we discovered that many single young adults attend the Later service, we provided monthly fellowship events to help this group develop a feeling of community. Our youth fellowship group also attends this service each week before their Sunday evening fellowship and learning activities. The Reverend Scanlan was a nightclub singer before going into parish ministry, and I maintain that she just cleaned up her nightclub act, brought it to church, and we call it Later@StLuke's!

Our Teaching Pastor and his team have started a midweek Bible teaching service called Word on Wednesday (WOW), which appeals to those persons who want to have more in-depth Bible study in the context of worship, music, and prayer. A lay couple in our congregation who have been inspired by Taizé worship experiences now lead a monthly Taizé service of music, scripture, silence, meditation, and prayer for those who desire a quiet meditative service.

Before starting multiple worship services, we discovered that St. Luke's was experiencing modest annual growth in our worship services. However, after starting multiple new services, we discovered a quantum leap in worship attendance. Ten years ago our average attendance was about 1,900 per week. Today it is more than 3,100 per week, and a large part of this increase is due to the increase in the number of worship opportunities provided.

I would encourage any size congregation to consider adding other types of worship services to reach new people who are not currently attending your worship services. If we only plan to reach those who are currently attending, we will only reach those like them who appreciate that particular type of worship. However, if we want to reach new groups of people with the good news, we have to be flexible enough to provide services that proclaim the gospel in language and forms they understand.

My prayer is that mainline congregations will become open enough to allow God to use them in reaching a wide variety of people with spiritual needs so that their lives can be transformed in worship by the good news of God's unconditional love, which comes to us in Jesus Christ.

CHAPTER 5

COMPASSIONATE CHANGE

E. CARVER MCGRIFF

L yle Schaller, in his book *Strategies for Change*, posed this question: "What is the number-one issue facing Christian organizations on the North American continent today?" His answer: "The need to initiate and implement planned change from within an organization. That is the number-one issue today for most congregations."[1]

Not every congregation seems open to change. Dr. Robert Hunter, a professional consultant with troubled Presbyterian churches, pointed out that some congregations are so socially inbred that their subconscious opposition to any growth beyond the addition of people who are "their own kind" prohibits any real progress. Often, as the elders of such churches die or otherwise become unable to attend, these churches either wither or simply reproduce their own kind.

Sometimes congregations hang onto their treasured past so tightly that any suggestions of change, especially if they come from some young pastor of short tenure who "doesn't appreciate the history and the culture of the congregation," are rejected out of hand. That pastor may then meet with inflexible resistance. Hunter explained that the underlying cause is one most congregants don't recognize in themselves: fear. In smaller congregations particularly, many people of long tenure with leadership roles can become jealous of their relative power and influence in the congregation and may see it threatened by change. This can lead to undercurrents of competition that are often ignited by the arrival of a new pastor who clearly doesn't know who's who and may, as some of the reigning leaders may fear, make some wrong decisions about leadership. If the pastor isn't patient and judicious, the choice of those who succeed in winning the pastor's early attention may lead to surprising coolness, even hostility, from those who were not so recognized or acknowledged.

Some churches are prone to internal dissension. In that event, the pastor may find it extremely difficult to effect any real change. It doesn't speak well for us Christians that these things are true, but we can go all the way back to the people of Corinth, to whom Paul wrote his treasured letters, to find that nothing has changed that much in human nature. "By the authority of our Lord Jesus Christ" he wrote, "I appeal to all of you, my brothers, to agree in what you say, so that there will be no divisions among you. Be completely united.... For some people from Chloe's family have told me quite plainly, my brothers, that there are quarrels among you" (1 Corinthians 1:10-11 GNT).

Let me suggest some things which I believe can enable a pastor to overcome most of this dissension and lead that congregation into a vital loving passionate ministry. We'll call them the *ten commandments for effecting change when some people don't want change*.

First, Look at Yourself

We must be fair to our people. How long have you been their pastor? Are you planning to remain there long enough to see things through, to live for a while with the consequences of any changes you might bring about? Have you considered what it feels like to worship in a church for many years, to have become comfortable there, to love that church and the many cherished memories located there, only to have someone from the outside arrive with ideas for change which may feel like disapproval of the past and present? Have you made every effort to understand the history of the people? Are you being sensitive to people's feelings and their right to reflect that long after you are gone they will still be there, living with your ideas? Have you prayed about your ideas, and have you sincerely discussed them with the people whose support you will need? If the answers to these questions are Yes! then it's time to proceed.

Second, Don't Solve the Problem from the Pulpit

There is a temptation to address divisive issues from the pulpit. Most of the leaders are present. The Bible is visible before them. Everyone has just said a wonderful prayer. Why not now? Because no matter how diplomatic you may feel yourself to be, some people will pick and choose among your words, will hear only what they want to hear, and the buzz which will follow outside your hearing can gain you only intensified opposition by those who already see you as on the side of the other people. Plus, it will seem an unfair advantage that you have a captive audience for your views with no opportunity for those who hold opposite views to express them. I'm not suggesting we refrain from upbeat discussions from the pulpit of future plans about which nearly everyone is convinced. It's certainly appropriate to explain those plans and details from the pulpit. But it's those controversies that preoccupy many church members, often outside the hearing of the pastor, which need to be dealt with in open discussions.

When I was the newly ordained pastor of my first church, I had a visiting minister preach for me while I was on a vacation. When I returned, I asked some elderly members how he did. One of them grumped to me that "all he talked about was politics." When I later heard his taped sermon, it contained one passing reference to the president. Some of the people present heard only that. That was all. Inform your people from the pulpit as things develop, but only after the dissension has been thoroughly dealt with behind the scenes. It's much wiser to discuss controversies where there can be open discussion.

Third, Take the Other People into Your Confidence

I recall once visiting the home of an older couple who were opposed to my desire to add a second unit to a small church I helped start in my early years. Preliminary plans had been drawn up showing some general ideas for the new unit. I spread the plans out on the floor of their living room and sprawled down beside them, then I said, "Hey you guys, come look at this." I went on at great length, displaying my own enthusiasm, pointing out the various advantages of the new unit. I invited their suggestions. I discussed options, and I talked about the benefits I saw to the plan without, however, acknowledging that I was aware of their opposition. Nor did they mention this. They ended the evening thinking the idea was great and supporting it enthusiastically in the congregation.

Every church has one or a few leaders whose quiet wisdom and personal qualities lead the rest of the congregation to be guided by their opinions. I had two such men in my early years at St. Luke's. One man in particular was pretty much the gate to any real change. He was very conservative but had the best interests of the church at heart. I made it a point to have lunch with the man frequently. When I had an idea for change I discussed it with him, making sure to let him know his opinion counted with me. If he disagreed with an idea I changed the subject, let him think about it for a while, then brought it up again. I knew that if he bought into the idea, felt he had in some way contributed to the process of thinking it through, he would give me his support. He nearly always did. And, looking back, the one or two ideas he did not support were not all that great after all.

Fourth, Don't Take Sides

When a plan for change is underway, disagreements can erupt between those who favor the plan and those who do not. While the senior pastor presumably favors the change, it doesn't follow that he or she will favor each and every voice in favor and oppose each and every voice against. Keep your eyes focused on the benefits to all the people. Side issues, age-old agendas, and even issues such as who gets to make the decisions, who has the authority around here, or how can we possibly consider undoing what old-what's-his-name did twenty years ago can surface. Unless these are moral issues about which you feel very strongly, by taking sides you can cause the opposition to unite against you. We do well to remember that we are pastor to all the church members, those with whom we disagree as much as those with whom we agree. Also, we're all human, and some people we find likable and some people we find disagreeable. It's easy to subconsciously side with those we like. We could be wrong. Once the congregation is polarized, the desired changes won't work anyway. The mark of a true pastoral leader is the ability to lead people to consensus. This takes patience and it takes diplomacy. But a divided congregation bodes ill for the pastor and, of course, for the congregation.

I'm not counseling cowardice. I have seen one or two church conflicts where the ethical issues were of such proportions as to demand a response by the pastor. But issues of such consequence are rare. Most are like the one I faced in my student church. For years the Easter sunrise breakfast had featured eggs and bacon, but a new group moved that the menu be changed to doughnuts and coffee. You can't imagine the rhubarb this produced. When asked, I said I liked both and please let me know what you decide. They kept the eggs and bacon, and I never heard any more about it. Once a pastor supports someone in a controversy he or she very probably alienates someone, maybe several someones, which at best undercuts the ability to be pastor and priest.

Fifth, Listen to the People Involved

It never ceases to amaze me how people respond when we listen attentively to what they have to say. The key is the ability to discern not only what a person is saying and thinking, but also what that person is *feeling*. I read just this past week about a representative of a telephone company who was assigned to try to collect a rather large bill from a recalcitrant customer who adamantly refused to pay. A customer service representative had already called on the man and utterly failed to collect. Litigation was in the offing. But the second man who called said something like this: "I know you feel we are being unfair. If I felt as you do I'd be angry too. Please tell me all about the problem." He then sat quietly and listened as the man first sputtered angrily about his feelings, then subsided, and remarkably, the man began to see that maybe he himself was being unfair. When his strong feelings had been thoroughly expressed, the man had become reasonable, and the situation ended with the man thanking the telephone company representative for listening, agreeing that maybe the bill was fair, and he wrote his check on the spot.

Stephen Covey sagely observed that "the greatest need of a human being is psychological survival—to be understood, to be affirmed, to be validated, to be appreciated." His prescription is what he calls empathic listening. "In empathic listening" Covey explains, "you listen with your ears, but you also, and more importantly, listen with your eyes and with your heart. You listen for feeling, for meaning. . . . You sense, you intuit, you feel."[2]

Sixth, Put Yourself in the Other Person's Place

This may be obvious, but it's remarkable how often we go into a tense situation with our own minds made up, not able to imagine why the other person feels as he or she does. One of the most effective things you can say to someone at a time of high dudgeon is *"If I were in your place I would feel exactly as you do."* That's true isn't it? If you were me you would feel as I do because you would be me. Once the dissident individual realizes you understand his or her feelings, you become an ally of sorts, even if you don't feel the same. This relaxes the tension and allows the other person to begin to listen to you also. One of the most imaginative, creative men I ever worked with was constantly thwarted in many of his attempted innovations, and it was for just one reason. He always sounded so sure of himself and bulled through with his own ideas so that other people subconsciously resisted them. There's a very important line between having strong convictions on the one hand and insisting on them to the point that those who initially disagree feel devalued and brushed aside on the other hand. Let the other person save face.

Seventh, Explain the Benefits to Everyone

Many years ago there was a famous salesman named Elmer Wheeler. He could sell about anything. He coined a phrase that was famous among salesmen for years. It went like this: "Don't sell the steak, sell the sizzle." I love that. Don't sell a church member on the new unit you want to build, sell him on the benefits to him and the church. Older people tend to oppose new building programs. Their children are grown, they like things the way they are, their incomes are down, and they're pretty sure you'll be coming after them if it flies. The building project is the steak. What is the sizzle? It's this: "Your children may live in another city. But somewhere, a congregation like ours is building a fine new Sunday School unit so your grandchildren there can have the same religious learning experience that you and your children had here. And someone is going to move here whose parents are in a church like this in some faraway place praying that their children will find a church whose members are willing to provide the facilities for their children to receive a great religious background as they grow up." That is true, it is genuine, and it is very persuasive with the older generation. Persuade people of the benefits to them and their loved ones of any changes, point out the ways in which the larger good will be served, and chances are, they'll enthusiastically support your ideas.

Eighth, Smile

I'm serious. It's amazing what a smiling good spirit can do to change another person's attitude. "Smile and the world smiles with you" my grandmother used to quote often. Several years ago, a friend of mine returned from a guided tour of Europe. He told me their guide, himself a European young man, said this to them: "Many Americans return from our country and tell people we are unfriendly. Let me tell you why. Americans never smile. Even though you're having a good time your faces are always grim. My people don't know you're having a good time. They think you don't like us, and no one likes someone they think doesn't like them. So, if you want to enjoy this trip, let's all smile." My friend, who had been on several previous tours, said everyone pasted big smiles on their faces wherever they went, and he said to me, "Carver, we had a great time. It made all the difference." Sometimes a church meeting seems fraught with tension. A genuine smile will often disarm the unhappy listener.

Ninth, Don't Argue

There's a time and place to take issue with someone when you disagree. To argue, however, usually causes the other person to plant his feet and remain firmer than ever. The leading teacher of human relationships, Dale Carnegie, whose classes in public speaking and self-improvement are famous today, wrote this about arguments. "I have listened to, engaged in, and watched the effect of thousands of arguments. As a result of all this, I have come to the conclusion that there is only one way under high heaven to get the best of an argument—that is to avoid it. Avoid it as you would avoid rattlesnakes and earthquakes."[3]

I learned the truth of this many years ago. I was a student doing post-seminary graduate work in a seminary. An award was given annually to the postgraduate student who, in the opinion of a group of professors, did the best work. I was a candidate for the award, had been led to believe I would receive it, and to be completely honest, I wanted it. One day toward the end of the semester, I visited the professor who was head of my committee of judges. I was a member of his class and had a straight A average. He made a small criticism of my work and I immediately began to argue with him. It went on for several minutes. I was absolutely sure I was right. He finally gave in and indicated that I should leave. A few days later I received my grades. He had given me a B, and needless to say, someone else received the award. I had departed in triumph but lost the argument.

We can all test this in our marriages. Marianne and I are very much in love. Ours is a mainly peaceful home. However, we both have strong personalities, and I have learned what I would dare guess many of you have learned. When I take time to quietly discuss some issue, everything runs smoothly. However, when I argue, the situation quickly becomes tense, a coolness settles over our relationship for a little while. More often than not when this happens, I go away wishing I had kept my mouth shut. But then it's too late. Arguing, as opposed to a quiet mutually listening discussion, never produces a good result in personal relationships. Remember the words of an obviously married poet:

> To keep your marriage brimming with love in the loving
> cup,
> Whenever you're wrong, admit it. Whenever you're
> right, shut up.

Tenth, Be There For Them

It's important to keep in mind that first, before anything else, as pastor I'm also priest. Our first responsibility in ministry is to care for the lost, the hurt, the poor, and the sometimes cantan-kerous person who may secretly be dealing with painful inner struggles. I have had times when I found myself putting my own agenda ahead of one or another person who really needed me to set that aside and care for her or him. I was always glad for those times when I rose to the occasion.

One of Methodism's most famous pastors from the past was Ernest Fremont Tittle, pastor of First Church in Evanston, Illinois. It was one of the three or four most prominent Methodist churches in America back in the 1940s. He was dearly loved. He was also controversial, being an ardent spokesman for racial equality, the poor, and a number of other causes not always pop-ular with the upscale residents of Evanston. One day a newspaper reporter was asked to do an interview with several members of the church to discern why, since Dr. Tittle was frequently on the wrong side of controversial issues according to his people, they still loved him. One member probably spoke for all when asked why, since his politics were so different from those of his pastor, he still wanted Tittle to remain, "He was there when my wife was sick. He was there with any one of us when we needed someone to encourage and care for us and love us. We know he loves us, and we can't imagine anyone else as our pastor." That's why we're there, isn't it? That's what ministry is all about.

During the latter part of the eighteenth century, the Quaker preacher John Woolman decided to do something about the problem of slavery. Many Quakers of the time were slaveholders, and Woolman believed this to be an abomination. However, he knew from observation that fiery oratory against the practice availed little against those who disagreed. So Woolman set out to visit every Quaker household where slaves were held. He traveled throughout the south and in the slavery-holding portions of the north. People knew, of course, of his opinions about slavery. However, his approach was friendly and non-confrontational. He would accept an invitation to remain for the night. In the course of the evening following dinner, the family would usually gather for good spirited conversation. Woolman would discuss many things, how farming was going in the region, what the children were learning, and only finally, the subject of slavery would arise. Woolman usually listened quietly as the host would talk. He would ask questions about the practice and especially how the Quaker faith fit in with slavery. Gently, without criticism, Woolman would press the issue until bedtime. The next morning, often leaving the discussion without closure, he would bid his hosts a cheery goodbye and be on his way.

John Woolman was practicing many of the principles we have discussed here. He listened, he was pleasant, he refused to argue, he made friends with his host family, and left on the most cordial possible terms. By the time of the Civil War not one Quaker family owned a slave.

Think about it. If you find yourself stymied as you seek to lead your congregation into a new tomorrow because there are people there who are opposed to your new ideas, consider what the outcome may be if you do these things. After taking an honest inward look to be sure your motives are pure and wise, go to your people without taking sides in any differences; just listen to their thoughts and their feelings; try to put yourself in their place; share with them your vision, but not aggressively; help them to see the benefits to them and their church; be pleasant in your demeanor, avoiding argumentation; and then there's a good chance your people will unite to support you. This is especially probable if they have already seen the signs of your love. When they feel your love, it will be returned and they will follow you.

Reflections on Chapter 5

M . K E N T   M I L L A R D

When I was a district superintendent, I gathered together all of the new pastors in my district for several orientation sessions as they came to serve their new congregations. Inevitably, they would begin to talk about how to make the changes in the order of worship they felt were needed in their new parishes. I discovered that there are at least two different schools of thought regarding how quickly to make worship changes or other changes when you arrive as pastor in a new congregation.

Some pastors maintain that a new pastor should make the changes they feel are necessary as soon as they arrive because the people of the congregation are expecting the new pastor to change things, and if he or she doesn't do it soon after arrival, people will think you like the old ways and it will make it harder to change things later. The "quick change" pastors would often quote some church consultants as authorities who supported their positions and would sometimes show us how they had radically changed the order of worship or something else on their first Sunday in the new congregation. They would often criticize their predecessor for their inadequate theology of worship and would bring in an order of worship that they felt was more theologically correct and which they personally preferred.

Another group of pastors believe that you should just accept the order of worship that is present when you arrive because it is what the people are used to, and after you've lived with it for a while, make changes slowly and with consultation with the leaders of the church. The "make changes slowly" pastors would also quote church consultants as authorities for their position and could tell stories about other pastors who were successful and long-tenured because they accepted things they may not have preferred out of love and respect for they people they were called to serve.

Carver has articulated well the stance that pastors should make changes slowly and only after listening to and consulting with the lay leadership of the congregation. Carver served St. Luke's for twenty-six years, retiring in June 1993. I arrived as senior pastor four months later in October 1993. I became aware of a lot of anxiety about my arrival and what changes I might seek to make in worship, staffing, and the overall direction of the congregation. This anxiety was expressed at my first staff meeting when a staff member asked if it was true that I was going to fire all of the staff and bring in a whole new staff. I explained that I belonged to the school of thought that said, "If it's not broke, don't fix it," and that it was clear to me that St. Luke's wasn't "broke" and in fact, was growing and changing lives in significant ways. I explained that my goal was to get acquainted with the people and culture of the congregation, to help continue the vital ministries that were already in place, and that any changes that were made would be in consultation with the staff and other leaders in the congregation.

The first test for me was the order of worship. The order of worship at St. Luke's was quite different from the order I was used to and preferred in my previous congregation. However, it was clear to me that the St. Luke's worship style was very meaningful to the vast majority of the congregation and to all of the other clergy staff and did, in fact, lead people to worship and praise God. I decided that it would be easier for me to change and learn to worship God in this different worship style than to require hundreds of people to change simply to make me more comfortable in worship. What has happened is that I have been converted and now prefer the St. Luke's style of worship more than what I was used to before. Looking back, I'm glad I didn't make any significant changes in worship when I first came! When new pastors come into congregations, I believe it is best to "go with the flow" for a while to see if God is seeking to change you or the congregation in any particular area of ministry.

Shortly after I arrived I discovered that people were often asking me, "Where are you going to lead us now?" I responded by telling people that it's not really about what I want for St. Luke's or, in fact, what they want. It's about what God wants for this congregation. I believe God has raised up St. Luke's, and every congregation, for God's purposes, and our goal as leaders is to discern God's desires for any particular congregation. Rather than our trying to enroll God in our desires and plans for the church, I believe God is trying to enroll us in God's desires and plans for our congregations.

But how do we discern where God is leading us? I believe that we can discern God's will for us as a congregation when we study the scriptures together, listen to the heartfelt needs of people in the congregation and in the community, and then surrender ourselves to God in prayer.

Shortly after I arrived at St. Luke's, I called together a visioning committee composed of anyone who wanted to attend and who would commit themselves to an early morning meeting every other week, where I would lead them in Bible study, ask them to tell me about various ministries of the church, and where we would pray to seek God's will for our congregation. I explained that God had just written a wonderful twenty-six-year chapter in the life of St. Luke's with the ministry of Carver McGriff, and now God was starting a new chapter, and our task was to discern where God was leading us.

After several months of studying scripture and praying together, we began to assess the needs of our congregation and the needs of our community. We conducted surveys in the congregation and surveys in the community to ascertain what God might be calling us to do next. We encouraged people to continue following their passions, and several new ministries emerged as a result of continuing to encourage and support passion driven ministries.

However, as a result of our surveys, we discovered that the biggest concern in the congregation was the lack of space for worship; lack of space for education for children, youth, and adults; and lack of space for adequate parking on Sunday mornings. People often reported that they would come to worship and if they couldn't find a place to park or a place in the sanctuary, they would return home because we had no space for them. One

Sunday our bishop attended a worship service and had to sit out in the narthex with about fifty other people looking at a brick wall and listening to the service over the public address system. After worship was over, I saw him and said, "Bishop, I didn't see you in worship today." He explained, "I wasn't exactly *in* worship. I was listening to it in the narthex with fifty other people."

Our mission at St. Luke's is to be "an open community of Christians gathering to seek, celebrate, live and share the love of God for all creation." Our Visioning Committee realized that if we did not have enough space for people to put their bodies in worship services, their children in church school, and to park their cars, we are not really an "open" community. We are, in fact, a "closed" community and are communicating to people that we are "full" and don't have a place for them to worship and grow in their faith here. As I mentioned earlier it was in response to this need that we started our first satellite service to help relieve some of our Sunday morning congestion. However, the congestion continued to increase on Sunday morning at our main campus.

Our Visioning Committee concluded that we needed to expand our worship, education, and parking space if we were to fulfill our mission as an "open" community of Christians. However, the Visioning Committee quickly divided into two opposing camps about how to meet our needs for additional space. One group maintained that we needed to relocate to a larger site in order to fulfill our mission, and they found such a site a few miles north of our present location. The other group maintained that we could expand our worship, education, and parking facilities on our current fourteen-acre site. One night the chairperson of our Visioning Committee asked for a "straw poll" to see how many people favored each position. We discovered that twenty were in favor of relocating and twenty were in favor of remaining where we were. I thought "Great! I've been here less than two years, and I've already divided the congregation in half!" I began to be filled with fear over what might happen because of the division in the congregation regarding relocation.

As a part of my own spiritual discipline, I seek to take one day each month for a personal spiritual retreat. I generally go to a nearby Catholic retreat center where I spend a day in silence, fasting, praying, studying Scripture, and journaling. The month after the "straw poll" I went on my spiritual retreat filled with fear. After a day of silence and seeking to surrender these concerns into the hands of God, I started to write in my journal. Three "words from the Lord" came to me, which I recorded in my journal that day. The first word was "Don't be afraid." I remembered that the first words of angels in many New Testament passages are "Don't be afraid." When the angel of the Lord appears to Mary, to Joseph, to the shepherds, or to the women at the tomb of Jesus, the angel's first words are "Don't be afraid." I realized that fear was my problem and that I needed to let go of fear and simply trust that God would lead us through this conflict over relocation.

The second word from the Lord was "Listen!" It reminded me to listen more than I talked; to listen for the "still, small voice of God," and to listen to all the other church leaders around me.

The third word was "Look for a sign." It was as if God was telling me that God would give us a clear sign telling us whether we should relocate or not and that I should stop worrying about it. Those three "words from the Lord" did not tell me what we were going to do but did tell me the process we needed to follow in seeking to discern God's will for our congregation.

At our next Visioning Committee meeting, I shared the three words from the Lord. Many people on our committee were also filled with fear because we were so divided over this issue, so I asked each person to let go of fear and replace it with trust that God would guide us in our decisions. I asked each person not to start any sentence with the phrase, "I'm afraid that..." because whatever followed would be coming from fear rather than faith.

Then I asked us to listen for God's still small voice giving us guidance and to listen to each other. We spent a long time sitting in quiet silence as we each sought to listen for the still small voice of God. Then I divided them into small groups of two people each with one being a person who wanted to relocate and the other being a person who wanted the church to expand in our current location. I asked one person to be the listener and to listen to the other person's position until they could articulate it back to them to their satisfaction. Then I asked them to reverse roles.

It was one of the best church meetings I have ever attended. The room was filled with genuine conversation, deep listening, and much laughter. Talking to each other one-on-one developed healing relationships and helped each person appreciate the other person and his or her faith and commitment to the church, even though they disagreed on this important issue. We discovered that even though we may not think alike, we can, indeed, love alike.

At the end of the evening, someone suggested that we needed architectural input before we could make this decision. They explained that those who wanted to relocate wanted to do so because they believed we could not build a 1600 seat sanctuary and additional educational space in our current location, while those who wanted to stay believed we could. It was explained that an architect could help us determine an answer to that question. A motion was made to hire an architect. It passed unanimously, and everyone concluded that "unanimous" is a good "sign" from the Lord as to what we should do.

An architect was hired, and he developed tentative architectural plans both for the current location and for the potential new site. These plans were shared with the Visioning Committee along with cost estimates for the expansion in each place. After seeing that we could, in fact, build sufficient facilities in our current location, the person who had led the charge to relocate made a motion to do our expansion at our current location with the provision that we purchase houses adjacent to our parking lot when they became available for sale to provide additional parking. That motion also passed unanimously, and we again felt that a unanimous decision out of a previously deeply divided committee was a good sign from the Lord that we were moving in the right direction.

Building plans were made, a capital campaign was held, and four years later we moved into a new 1600-seat sanctuary and provided increased educational space for children and adults, new music facilities, a prayer chapel, spiritual life center, and expanded parking.

Attendance in worship and education immediately increased about 30 percent, and we were able to start reaching more people with the good news of Jesus Christ.

In addition to following the processes for change outlined by Carver earlier in this chapter, we also sought to be very intentional in being open to where God was seeking to lead us. Sometimes personality conflicts and power issues arise when a pastor proposes change in a congregation, but when the pastor and other leaders recognize that the goal is to discern together the will of God for the congregation, it changes the whole mood and atmosphere. It's not about whether the pastor gets her or his way or whether certain leaders in the congregation get their way; rather, it's about whether God's way is present in the congregation. We need to continually remember Jesus' prayer in the Garden of Gethsemane, "O God, not my will, but thine be done."

In his book, *Discerning God's Will Together,* Danny Morris uses an illustration I have found helpful in enabling groups to discern the will of God together. Danny asks us to imagine that at the center of every group there is a huge prism. If there were a light shining down on that prism, it would reflect that light differently to each person present. Each person would see the reflected light that came to them, but no one would see all of the light coming into the prism. In a similar way, every issue is like a prism at the center of the group, and everyone has some light to share about that issue, but no one sees all the light there is. Therefore, whenever a group is seeking to discern God's will on any issue, they need to allow every person to share the light they see, to respect the light others see, and to keep turning the prism until everyone sees a brighter light. This process may take longer than simply voting on issues, but it respects and values each person present and results in decisions that are broadly supported and may reflect more closely the desires of God for the congregation.[4]

I also suggest that if we want to discern the will of God, surrender comes before knowledge. By this I mean that we need to surrender to the will of God before we will know it. Normally, we want God to tell us God's will for us or for our congregation, and then we will decide whether or not we want to do it. However, God will not play that game with us because it means we are trying to be "God" in our own lives—we are still in charge and making our decisions on the basis of what we think is in our own best interests. When we say to God that we surrender ourselves into God's hands and will do whatever God calls us to do, then, and only then, will we discover God's will and desires for us.

Father Charles DeFoucauld, in his book *Meditations of a Hermit*, teaches us a prayer of surrender which I believe puts us in a position to hear and discern the will of God for ourselves: "My Father, I commend myself to you, I give myself to you, I leave myself in your hands. My Father, do with me as you wish. Whatever you do with me, I thank you."[5]

John Wesley invited his followers to offer a similar prayer of surrender when he encouraged them to pray:

> I am no longer my own but thine. Put me to what thou wilt, rank me with whom thou wilt. Put me to doing, put me to suffering. Let me be employed by thee or laid aside for thee, exalted for thee or brought low by thee. Let me be full, let me be empty. Let me have all things, let me have nothing. I freely and heartily yield all things to thy pleasure and disposal. And now, O glorious and blessed God, Father, Son and Holy Spirit, thou art mine, and I am thine. So be it. And the covenant which I have made on earth let it be ratified in heaven. Amen.[6]

Unfortunately, many times when we pray, we are trying to enroll God in our desires and recruit God to help us get what we've already decided we want. However, the truth about life is that God is trying to enroll us in accomplishing God's will for the world. Actually, we should not be asking, "What is God's will for me or for my congregation?" We should be asking, "What is God's will?" period. What is God's will for the whole world and how is God trying to enroll me and my congregation in accomplishing it? We should be asking, "Where is God demonstrating unconditional love, forgiveness, hope, faith, and transformation in the world?" and "How is God seeking to get us involved in these life transforming ministries?"

I believe that when we surrender control of our lives and of our congregations into the hands of God then we will discover the changes which God is seeking to make in us, in our congregations, and in the world around us.

CHAPTER 6

HEROES IN THE SANCTUARY

E. CARVER MCGRIFF

I was a high school student as World War II was bursting into flame and the Japanese had bombed Pearl Harbor. One of my vivid memories is of the posters that soon appeared in every U.S. Post Office showing Uncle Sam, sometimes attired in his familiar red white and blue, sometimes coatless with his sleeves rolled up. In each picture his finger was pointed at the viewer, and underneath, the motto read: "Uncle Sam wants you." His stern countenance made it clear that a grim purpose was afoot. All over America, young men and many young women, called out to serve, were lining up at recruiting stations to join one of the armed forces. Two of my closest friends, still high school juniors, dropped out of school and joined the Navy. In spite of all the dangers that clearly lay ahead, men and women of America could hardly wait to take their places in the service of their country. Talk to most older Americans about those days, and after they solemnly describe the many privations of the time, nearly all will end up by remembering those as exciting, in many ways romantic, days of high adventure.

There's something of that in nearly all of us, some rush of the red blood of heroism, a deep, God-given urgency in time of crisis, to rise to the occasion of some great need. We have only to be called out, to be challenged by the impossible. I truly believe that seated before those of us who preach the gospel are crowds of heroes. We have only to issue the summons and convince them we will stand alongside them in the work ahead. I am a firm believer in the truth of those well-remembered words of President Theodore Roosevelt:

> Far better it is to dare mighty things, to win glorious triumphs, even though checkered by failure, than to take rank with those poor spirits who neither enjoy much nor suffer much, because they live in the gray twilight that knows not victory nor defeat.[1]

These are days when we Christians who would see the church arise in new life must, ourselves, heed the call to sacrifice.

> Jesus calls us oe'r the tumult of our life's wild, restless sea;
> day by day his sweet voice soundeth, saying "Christian, follow me!"[2]

Today's younger generations need to be reminded that during the civil rights era in America the people of the churches rose up and endured the conflicts of change and the inner battles of their own souls, to enable a dramatic new era in race relationships. During the conflict in Southeast Asia it was the clamor of outraged, Christian voices, many parading in front of government facilities, at times reviled by countrymen who still disagreed with such opposition, which finally convinced President Johnson to call off the war in Vietnam before yet more young men died in a tragically unwinnable war. In times of crisis the people of the cross will always be there and counted when the cause is just and the way is known. It's the church, and that means those of us who presume to be its leaders, who must issue the call and lead the way as together we prepare for the cross, the price by which the new day in the church can be ushered in.

Stephenson, in his classic, *God in My Unbelief*, which is regrettably out of print, said it well:

> If we look for the kind of peace which will leave us as we are we shall find that it is not to bring that kind of peace that Christ has come but with a sword to pierce it. If we wish to be comforted and assured that, because there is forgiveness, we can rest in what we have made of ourselves, we shall encounter Him who will not let us rest.[3]

So what's the point? Won't this kind of summons to expensive service cause our churches to decline? Isn't this the "me generation," the people so immersed in spending and acquiring and possessing that to sound this call flies in the face of everything Americans value today? Isn't the present search for spiritual renewal premised on the comfort of God, free of costly sacrifice? Yes, this indictment is not without its truth. But all generations have that rich heroic blood coursing through their veins. They have only to be called out, challenged. It was my experience that people, especially younger members, wanted to hear this call to service. Not everyone steps forth of course, but most people want to believe their congregation is relevant to the needs of the world and, closer, to their own community. I believe a new day is dawning in America. We're tired of superficial values. September 11 has awakened the hero within a whole generation of young people who want something better from themselves. Peter Gomes who works with outstanding young emerging leaders as professor of Christian morals at Harvard University, recently wrote this optimistic appraisal:

> Somehow, and with little help from their elders, our young people, particularly in our schools, colleges, and universities, have begun to discover those truths that last in time of need. Unbeknownst to much of the profit-

driven mavens of a corrosively materialistic popular culture that preys on the susceptibilities and anxieties of
youth, these very same youth…have been on a search for
greatness, for goodness, and even for nobility, that more
excellent way of life of which Saint Paul speaks.[4]

Many Christians want to do something relevant, something
that really matters. The church's role is to discern the needs and
present them with such clarity as to enable me, as I sit there in
worship, to see what I might do to make that difference, and to
call me out to action. Maybe I can't change the current plight of
the Hispanic immigrant, or the unemployed young black man, or
the abused child. Maybe I can't reverse today's moral indifference
and blatant consumerism all at once. But I can do something,
something important, something that makes a difference. To
begin with, I can open my mind to understand the plight of people who haven't had the advantages in life which I take for
granted. I can allow my heart to be opened to the fears, the broken spirits, the dark tunnel of life ahead which beckons to so
many people whose lives are so usually lived outside my little
framework of existence, and I can witness to this to my friends.
I can share my wealth, help to underwrite the many church-
sponsored ministries to those in such heart-breaking, life-spoiling
need. And I can employ what God-given gifts are mine in the
service of laudable causes, whether to wield a hammer on a
Habitat For Humanity building project, or spend my
Thanksgiving morning serving food at the homeless shelter, or
lead a workshop on parenting or on grief recovery. Maybe I can
teach a Sunday school class. Whatever my gifts, my worldly treasure, I can share. And I as pastor can stand up and try to be the
person I call other people to be.

Here's the point. People want to know where to start, where to
make a difference. But one essential point needs to be made, one
we all know deep down but so easily forget. When it comes to
specifics in church life, *someone must ask me.* Maybe it shouldn't
be that way, but we're talking reality here, and that's the way it
is. When we announce a project of one kind or another to help

others and we ask for volunteers, we'll get a few. But when we say to an individual, face to face, "Will you help?" people respond. I have twice in recent years gone to Jamaica on work projects sponsored by St. Luke's Church. Both times I thought about it, and decided not to go. I think a wrench is something you use to drive a nail. Both times I went because the leader came to me and said, "Carver, we need you on this project. Will you come?"

If we want to enlist people in the work of the Lord, we must go to them, ask them, invite them. Too often we announce grand plans from the pulpit then stand back while that small contingent of people who always do, steps forth yet again, while the great majority of our people go home, reflect that "maybe I ought to get involved in that" but by the time Sunday brunch is over and the NFL game is started, the thought is gone. I have observed that nearly all the men and women, and I should add, many teenagers, who are leading our churches are people who, at some point in time were asked one on one, "Will you?"

This is a splendid time in which to live. These are exciting times. Change is afoot. A new generation of young people is ready to be called out. What a shame if in times like these we Methodists allow ourselves to be left on the sidelines while God is calling young people to throw off the enervating values of self-interest and promiscuity and to embrace his promise of saving power and his call to the supremely satisfying ethic of servitude to love. Paul said it so well: "And if the man who plays the bugle does not sound a clear call, who will prepare for battle?" (1 Corinthians 14:8 GNT). If your church is to grow, if God is to enable your success in this effort, it will be in large part because of your clear and specific call to action.

What about the people in the congregation who are struggling with marriage problems, with illnesses, with failures and guilt and broken dreams and addictions and hopes as yet unrealized? Doesn't all this overlook those universal hurts to which Jesus addressed himself again and again, our own personal troubles which need tending to? What about those needful souls whose pain or disability right now calls for kindly caring? Obviously if Sunday after Sunday the people hear a steady diet of demanding challenges, as though the preacher is oblivious to the human situation, people will get tired and some will leave. But a steady diet of reassurance and kindly promises of forgiveness without the cross at the heart of the message will breed weakness and self-centered religion, and it won't be faithful to the gospel. Often the antidote to my debilitating problem is to devote myself to some worthy undertaking which pulls me out of myself, takes my mind off me, and directs it toward what Jesus Christ's calling is all about.

Flo Spear recently learned she is to die soon. *The Indianapolis Star* newspaper told her story the other day. Her body scarred by endless surgeries, her days so often darkened by dialysis, hardly able to rise from her bed with loving help, her mind sometimes tortured with memories of an abusive marriage, Flo is the life of the party. Hospital people visit her to have their spirits revived. Flo, soon to leave us as she well knows, has daily visits from her many friends from St. Luke's Church and welcomes them all. John Shaughnessy, feature writer for *The Star*, after spending an hour with Flo told her she was the most inspiring person he had ever interviewed. Not long ago Flo appeared on Dave Letterman's show. Dave gave Flo a big hug at the end, and when he was informed that Flo was raising money for the battered women's home, he sent a donation and asked that the amount be secret. However, Flo slipped during her interview with Shaughnessy and told that the amount was five thousand dollars. She quickly caught herself, tried to stop, but it was too late. So she said, "What the hell, I'll be dead anyway. Let 'em sue me."

The other day Flo had her seventy-seventh birthday party in her managed care room. She said seven was her lucky number and with two of them together she was sure to have a good day. She called it her going-away party and invited all her many friends to attend but with the proviso that each must contribute a hundred dollars to be given to the home for battered women. She asked that her possessions be auctioned now while she was around. When her nephew said they wouldn't get much for them, Flo informed him, "What do you mean worth nothing? I just sold one hundred two-dollar lunches for a hundred dollars each." People who attended said it was a blast.

Defeated? Not on your life. Flo, who has suffered a lot in her years, in constant pain, continually exhausted, is ready and somewhat excited to see what's next. Pain, illness, debilitation, even imminent death, these haven't gotten her down because she is always thinking about other people. Flo showed what service to others can do for the one who serves, even in time of personal crisis. At last report, Flo, in her dying hours, has already raised more than $22,000 for the charity of her heart. And Flo? She was grinning from ear to ear when last seen—in church. The call to a high-minded worthy life, one that exemplifies the qualities of love and honor, will unfailingly win the loyalty of our people every time. Our job is to issue the call to action. (Shortly after this was written, Flo passed on to her next great adventure.)

There is, of course, another side to this. Having said that the summons to a life of gallant service lies at the heart of our faith, it's also true that on any given Sunday we are addressing many people who are already saints of far greater commitment than we who preach. And many are in dire need of a healing, comforting word. Lyle Schaller recorded that "the one theme that is common to churches that are attracting more people is the theme of hope."[5] That hope lies in two directions, the inward knowledge of God's constant action in our lives and the outward actions in our own lives as we do the work we are called to do. French mystic Teilhard de Chardin wrote: "It is in free and loving service to his fellow men that the individual finds himself, finds the world, and finds God."[6] Stephenson saw this for the whole church. "This is the paradox which is at the heart of the Church's existence: that only a Church which is so involved in the world that it cries out in despair because of its involvement, and is even shaken in its own faith, can be the means of saving the world."[7] People need to hear this word of hopeful promise.

Jesus said "Come to me all who labor and are heavy laden, and I will give you rest." So Jesus was addressing two aspects of the human condition. Sometimes we are ready to be challenged, to be called out of ourselves to the highest and best of which we are capable. But sometimes, when we are heavy laden, hurting, exhausted beyond our capacities, overwhelmed, we need compassionate understanding help. Most of us have quoted the adage which I believe originated in the newspaper business, but it applies to the Church: "Our role is to comfort the afflicted and afflict the comfortable." I've been in both situations, and you have too. The pastor who is able to discern and speak to both situations at the proper time in the proper way will be the most effective gospel messenger.

A beloved professor at Christian Theological Seminary in Indianapolis taught the Bible. He loved to tell of the time he was a freshman in a church-related college, and being innocent where girls were concerned, he was very inexperienced in the department of romance. One day a senior student asked him to double date for the Spring dance with the two daughters of the university president. It seems that the president did not yet permit his girls to single date, and the freshman was being pressed into service for the occasion so the senior could date the older girl to whom he was attracted.

The evening went surprisingly well, and as curfew time drew near the two young men were escorting the girls home on a darkened path which passed along a charming stream, by several towering oak trees. The freshman, much smitten with his young date, made a very important decision. He decided that when they passed a large oak tree hidden up ahead in the darkening shadows, he would take the young lady by the arm, gently draw her behind the tree, and give her a goodnight kiss. The moment drew near. He slowed to let the other couple draw ahead, and with racing pulse as they arrived at the oak tree, he gently took his young lady by the arm. But just as he was going into action, the senior student turned around, faced the two of them, and there in the moonlight suggested, "Shall we have a prayer before we say goodnight?" Relating the story much later, the professor said "I'm a firm believer in prayer, but there's a time and place for it and that wasn't it."

Timing, even in religious matters, is important. As preachers we must strike a wise and firm balance between the call to action on behalf of others and the assurance of comfort in time of personal need. To fail in either is to ensure an unhealthy church.

This, then, is the role of the wise preacher, to issue frequent reminders of Jesus' admonition that "anyone who would come after me let him take up his cross," yet never fail to keep uppermost in every worshiping mind that invitation to "come unto me all who labor and are heavy laden and I will give you rest." Just as we parents want our kids to live happy, healthy lives and, at the same time, be people of courage and devotion who live for something beyond themselves, so God must surely have the same hope for us. The skill, of course, lies in the means by which this message is broadcast, the spirit in which it issues from the preachers mouth—and life. And of course, to remain with the child-parent analogy, if we see any of our kids in distress, we drop everything and run to them. So with God. This is the promise people need to hear, and they will come to hear it.

The other evening we had some guests in our home as their two beautiful twin children celebrated their fifth birthday. Little Sarah told us that the other day she heard her mother say to a friend, "You're my sister in Christ." Then Sarah looked at me, smiled, and said "Carver, you're my brother in Christ." Out of the mouths of babes. We're all in this together and what a gift to give the persons who comes into our midst, to declare them our sister, our brother, our friend "in Christ."

There must be some reason why so many nondenominational congregations are growing rapidly while traditional congregations are in a slow state of decline. Two reasons seem clear to me. We are too often failing to awaken the hero within, and we are not succeeding in reaching into the lives of those people outside our ranks with the saving and healing word and work of Jesus Christ. In too many cases, our efforts are ineffective and our worship is not stimulating for a Walkman-bound, MTV-educated, computer-literate generation of fine young men and women who are searching for the meaning and the fulfillment of their lives.

It's in the acting out of these sentiments, the call to service and the reaching out ministries, both performed in such personal ways as to address clearly everyone in the congregation (member, constituent and—here's an important key—visitor), that soon spreads the word to far-away places that this is a church where God is truly at work.

A well-known preacher told of a Methodist church whose pastor noticed that a woman who had been an active member had been absent for a long time. He recalled that her husband had died a year or so earlier. So in good preacherly fashion, he found time to drop by the woman's home to inquire about her absence. It seems that, with some embarrassment, the woman reported that following the death of her husband, some ladies of her church had made a routine call, expressed their condolences, asked her to call if there was anything they could do to help, and that was the final contact. But a group of women from a nearby Catholic church had learned of her sadness. They had brought meals for her several growing children. They had made arrangements for someone to baby sit half a day each week so she could get away from home. And, through the year, they stayed in close touch to help. So, she explained, although she admitted some problems with the theological teachings of the Catholics, she had become a member there and was now learning about their faith. Those people had been little Christs to a suffering woman and she was finding him. There, in a nutshell, is what the church is all about: serving people, sacrificing for each other. Issue the call, many will respond. Churches grow when we do this.

Now I want to make what I consider a crucially important point, one which goes contrary to the practices of many fast growing, but very conservative congregations. I advocate welcoming people into membership who are *not yet ready* to affirm Jesus Christ as Lord. There are two ways to view the church, as I see it. One, it is a community of people who acknowledge the Lordship of Jesus Christ over all the earth. But the church can also be that place where people go to make the journey, which eventually leads to the recognition and acceptance of Christ as Lord. I sometimes talk to people who joined St. Luke's Church many years ago, people whose reasons for joining ranged from cooperation with a spouse, to "I suppose my kids ought to be in Sunday school," to "Something's missing in my life and I thought

I'd try you folks for an answer." And some say that long since, Christ has claimed their loyalty. John (not his real name) joined because his friends all attended there and his wife wanted to attend a church. He was an infrequent attendee, but he developed a sense of loyalty to the community. Then he developed cancer. Today John is a devout believer, credits Jesus Christ for his courageous battle with the disease, and now that it has been in remission for several years, he is an inspiring leader of a Bible study group in the church. He was there when the time was right for conversion.

Paul wrote "So faith comes from what is heard, and what is heard comes through the word of Christ" (Romans 10:17). Obviously, if we can attract someone to the setting where Christ is preached, it is there better than in any other setting, that the Holy Spirit can do his work. Wise is the preacher, then, who welcomes anyone who will to come to be part of the congregation.

I don't see people as suddenly moving from doubt to belief, as though stepping across some invisible line to become part of the in group. Rather, each is in his or her own place along the journey. Many a "converted Christian" is still a major pain in the neck while many a frankly struggling nonbeliever displays marvelous kind love. You and I can't know who suffered what in the early years of life that may have tainted and colored the religious outlook of an individual, nor what private tortures may mar their lives today.

Only God can judge among us, and our work is to draw all whom we can reach by any of a variety of enticements into the hearing of the Word. When this welcome is known, many people who are not by any means ready to sign on the dotted line will come to listen. That's all I ask. We who are there can then go to work to give an assist to the Spirit, not only by what we say but also by how we live and how we treat them and each other. When a congregation intentionally acts this way, the word gets around, and even people not nearly ready to call themselves devout Christians will come to become part of the community. There, in a passion driven congregation such as that, the One who loves us most of all awaits.

Reflections on Chapter 6

M . KENT MILLARD

Carver has talked about the leaders of the church calling out the heroic in the heart of every person. I would like to talk about the leaders of the church calling the congregation to heroic giving and generosity for the sake of transforming our world into a compassionate, inclusive, Christ-like community.

After the St. Luke's congregation had decided to expand our facilities in our current location, the concern was how we would ever be able to raise sufficient funds to build the facilities that were needed. I suspect many congregations have the experience where someone will say: "It's a great idea, but we just can't afford it; we don't have the money." Consequently, many God-inspired ministries and ideas never see the light of day because of our conversation that "we can't afford it" and "the people of this congregation do not have a history of generous giving."

It was estimated that we would need to raise at least $12 million to provide a new sanctuary seating 1,600 people, a new education and music building, a Spiritual Life Center and Prayer Chapel, and expanded parking. The congregation had never raised more than $1.2 million in the past in any capital expansion program, and many people predicted that we would never be able to raise the necessary funds for this expansion.

I asked people if they believed it would be a miracle if we raised enough funds to build these new facilities, and everyone said, "Yes! It would be a miracle if this congregation ever gave that much." I suggested that we entitle our campaign "Expect a Miracle." I invited all of our leaders to believe that God is still working miracles in the world and that God could work the miracle of generosity in our congregation if God chose to do so.

I discovered that getting Christians to believe that miracles are still possible is the hardest part. We have become so logical, rational, and controlling that it is difficult for us to believe that God is still active, powerful, and leading the church which Christ brought into being. We tend to believe it is *our* church and we are in control, rather than seeing it as *God's* church and believing God is in control. When anyone asked our leaders if they believed we could raise the necessary funds for this expansion, I coached them to respond simply by saying, "It's possible," and it was hard for many to say even those words. We didn't know if God was going to work the miracle of generosity here or not, but I simply wanted people to believe and to articulate that it is possible.

In Matthew 13 we are told about an occasion when Jesus returned to his own hometown of Nazareth, preached in his home synagogue, and people were astounded at his wisdom and power. They couldn't believe that this Jesus whom they had watched grow up in his father's carpenter shop and had become a carpenter himself was now offering words of divine insight and performing miracles. They said, "Where did this man get this wisdom and these deeds of power? Is not this the carpenter's son? Is not his mother called Mary?...Where then did this man get all this? And they took offense at him." Then Matthew concludes this section with this significant comment: "And he did not do many deeds of power there, because of their unbelief" (Matthew 13:54-58).

Jesus did not do many deeds of power or miracles in Nazareth because the people of Nazareth did not believe that he could perform deeds of power or miracles. Jesus performed miracles in the nearby towns of Cana and Capernaum, but he did not perform miracles in his own hometown "because of their unbelief." Undoubtedly there were blind, disabled, and sin-sick persons in Nazareth just as there were in these other communities, but they were not healed because of the unbelief of the people of Nazareth. I've often wondered about the hurting and wounded people of Nazareth who were not healed simply because they did not believe that Jesus had the power to work miracles. I also wonder about the miracles that do not occur in our congregations and communities because of our unbelief. Jesus may be longing to perform certain miracles among us, but they do not happen because of the unbelief of Christian leaders.

In our secular society people often say that they won't believe it until they see it, but I like to turn that around and say they won't see it until they believe it. Belief comes first, and when we begin to believe in miracles and expect them, then perhaps we will begin to see miracles happening all around us.

I first learned the power of expecting miracles in generosity when I was pastor at First United Methodist Church in Sioux Falls, South Dakota. The congregation had just completed a capital funds campaign and built a new educational addition and installed a new pipe organ. After it was all over we still had about $200,000 in indebtedness. Our finance committee was reluctant to conduct another capital campaign, so I suggested we just take a special offering one Sunday, receive $200,000 and pay off the debt. The finance committee looked at me as if I was crazy. This was a congregation of about 2,200 members with a modest history of giving, and they said there was no way the congregation would ever give that much on one Sunday. Again, I asked them if they believed it would be a miracle if that happened, they agreed it would, so I suggested we call it "Miracle Sunday."

We set "Miracle Sunday" on Palm Sunday that year, and all during Lent we talked about how God is still working miracles in the world today. During one Sunday morning service I interviewed a young couple who had been married for ten years and were told over and over by many doctors that they would never be able to conceive and bear a child. As they told that story, they were holding their three-month-old daughter in their arms, and they cried as they gave their thanks to God and said "It's a miracle." Another Sunday I interviewed a man who had been told that he had terminal cancer and had only about a year to live, but he was told that eight years earlier and now appeared in excellent health. Whenever he visited his doctor he was told there was no medical reason for him to still be alive, and the man concluded by simply saying "It's a miracle." Of course, not every infertile couple conceives and not every cancer patient is healed, but the fact that it happens sometimes ought to keep us open to the possibility that God is still working miracles in the world.

I asked the congregation to do three things during Lent. First, to believe that the miracle of generosity was possible; second, to pray about it and give whatever they felt God wanted them to give; and third, to accept whatever miracle God wanted to give. Our chief unbeliever was the chair of our finance committee. He said that he knew well the giving patterns of our congregation and that there was no way the church would give that much money on one Sunday. He supported the project because he believed whatever was given would help reduce our indebtedness, but he was sure we wouldn't reach our goal. However, about a week before Miracle Sunday he called to tell me something was happening to him; he was starting the believe it might be possible for us to reach that goal in one Sunday. The miracle had already started to happen because another person had moved from unbelief to faith.

A woman who was a member of a Lutheran church heard about our Miracle Sunday project and sent a very generous check with the note, "I've always wanted to be a part of a miracle." A Baptist pastor called the week before Miracle Sunday and told me he and his congregation would be praying for us on that Sunday because "the world needs more miracles." When Miracle Sunday arrived, I told the congregation that a Lutheran woman had sent a generous gift and a Baptist church was praying for us and that when a United Methodist congregation has Lutheran gifts and Baptist prayers, a miracle has already happened!

The Miracle Sunday offering was received early in each service, taken out and counted, and at the end of the third service, our lay leader came gliding down the center aisle with a glow on her face and a slip of paper in her hand which she gave me. On the paper was written the number, "$210,000" indicating that $210,000 in cash and checks had been given on Miracle Sunday! When I told the congregation the good news they applauded and wept as we sang, "To God be the glory for the things He has done." Our hearts were filled full to overflowing with thanksgiving and gratitude to God because it was clear to all of us that God had been at work in the hearts of people to engender this kind of generosity on one Sunday.

Everyone wondered how it came out right at the number we needed when no one had any idea what anyone else was giving. We discovered that people who had no record of giving gave generously because they were inspired by the vision and wanted to "do it once for God." All we could say is: "It must be a miracle" because we had no logical answer for all the questions raised.

The most important aspect of Miracle Sunday was not the funds raised but the faith raised. More people began to attend Bible study classes, prayer meetings, and worship services because they felt they had been in the presence of a real miracle of God.

I shared that story with our St. Luke's congregation to inspire persons to "Expect a Miracle," and miracles started to happen all around us. A building committee of about fifteen persons had been appointed and was working on the detailed plans for the new facilities. At one of the meetings our lay leader, who is a professional fundraiser and coordinated our fundraising activities, told our building committee that each one of us needed to make a personal commitment to the campaign before we presented the proposal to the congregation. She handed out slips of paper and asked each of us to write down what we expected to give. They were collected, totaled, and then she announced that the building committee of fifteen people had just committed over one million dollars to the campaign! Everyone was shocked and surprised at the generosity around the table, and we could only say to each other, "It's a miracle."

God worked the miracle of generosity in the hearts of many others in the congregation as well. One day a man that I barely knew called and left a message on my voice mail machine. He explained that he and his wife had decided to give one million dollars to our Expect a Miracle campaign. He left it on my voice mail! I listened to that message over and over to make sure I understood what he had said. Then I called to thank him for his gift and to invite him and his wife out to lunch. I told him that we give a free lunch to everyone who gives a million dollars!

Professional fundraisers tell us that large gifts usually come from long-time, well-established leaders in the congregation. However, this man and his family did not fit that profile. They were newer members of the church, they held no leadership positions in the congregation, and they were not known by any of the leaders of the congregation. They simply said they appreciated the worship services on Sunday and loved the Christian education experience their children were receiving in church school and wanted to do all they could to help the church move forward.

Another miracle happened one Sunday after worship. We knew that the new organ for the new sanctuary would cost about $600,000, and we didn't know where the funds would come from for it. Our music director kept asking me if we had the funds for the new organ, and I kept saying, "God hasn't made that clear yet." One Sunday after worship a couple came out of church and simply said, "Put us down for the organ!" I said, "$600,000?" They said "Yes" and gave the funds for a magnificent organ that is used to lead and inspire us in worship every week.

Another Sunday a little ten-year-old boy came up to me with a brown paper bag filled with coins. His parents explained that he had been saving his allowance for months to help build the new church and he wanted to give it to me personally. When he put the heavy, coin-filled bag in my hands, I asked him why he was doing this. He simply answered, "I want to do my part to help." I saw a look of love and joy in his face that I will never forget. I believe it's also a miracle when a ten-year-old boy chooses not to use his allowance for video games or toys for himself but to give it to God's work through his congregation.

I firmly believe that one of the reasons we don't see more miracles in our congregations is because we as leaders do not expect miracles to happen. And they don't! In a way similar to what happened in Nazareth, Jesus does no mighty works among us because of our unbelief. Many congregations may not have members with the kind of resources to give million-dollar gifts, but every congregation has members who could be far more generous in sharing their resources with God's work if the leaders modeled generosity themselves and expected the miracle of generosity to occur in their own congregation.

In our first phase capital campaign entitled Expect a Miracle, we set a goal of receiving $7.5 million in pledges for our new facilities. However, by the end of the campaign we had received over $8.5 million in pledges and gifts. I believe it happened because the congregation had been enrolled in the vision of expecting miracles. In the second phase of the campaign entitled, "With God, All Things Are Possible," we received another $5.5 million in pledges, which are currently being received and used to pay mortgage payments on our new facilities and provide for additional expansion. God is so faithful to us; the challenge is for us to be faithful and trusting totally in God to continue to work whatever miracles God wants to work.

The first year we moved into our new facilities, worship and church school attendance jumped about 30 percent and has continued to increase about 12 percent each year. Our goal is to reach a critical mass of people in our community with the good news of Jesus Christ so that our society might be transformed; expanding our worship and educational space has allowed us to move toward that critical mass goal.

Sometimes leaders are afraid that if the congregation gives generously to a capital campaign, it will harm mission-giving or giving to the annual budget. However, we have discovered that the opposite is the case. During the time of the capital campaign and the building of the new facilities, the giving for mission projects increased about 20 percent each year and the annual budget increased by about 12 percent each year. When people invest generously in new facilities, they also want to make sure that funds are necessary to support the programs that will take place in those new facilities, and they want to care for the needs of those beyond the walls of the church.

Furthermore, they also discover there is a deep joy in giving generously to God. Life is made in such a way that it is circular. We all receive life as a generous gift from God, then we give generously back to God to say thanks, and then we receive again, and we give again. When we receive gifts from God and try to hoard them for ourselves alone, we stop the flow of generosity, and we die spiritually and personally. The human heart is an analogy of this process. Our hearts receive blood from the rest of our body and then pump it out again to all the other organs in our bodies. If our hearts only received the blood and tried to hoard it all for itself, we would die. Our hearts receive and give; receive, and give over and over again. That is how our lives are maintained. In a similar way, we receive all of life as a gift from God, and we need to give back our time, talent, and treasure to God out of gratitude. Then we receive again, and we are inspired to give again and again.

I have discovered that many pastors and church leaders are uncomfortable talking to their congregations about giving. They seem to believe that talking about giving is a bad thing to do and hurts their people. However, the opposite is the case. Giving people an opportunity to give to God's work is giving them an opportunity to be blessed. I have had numerous people tell me that once they got over their inhibitions against generous giving they experienced blessings in their lives in ways they could never have anticipated. Our motive for giving is not so that we'll be blessed, but the truth about life is that when we open up and give generously to God, we are, in fact, blessed in numerous ways. Jesus was not afraid to talk about money and giving to God. Some scholars estimate that about 50 percent of the teachings of Jesus have something to do with surrendering ourselves and our resources to God.

Teaching people to give is also an antidote to greed. Jesus said, "Take care! Be on your guard against all kinds of greed" (Luke 12:15). Greed is obviously one of the persistent sins of our generation and is destroying the lives of many people around the world. At a time when the greed of chief executive officers and other officials in large corporations is destroying life and hope for many people around the world, we recognize clearly the damage that ego-centered greed is causing in our lives. The antidote to greed is generosity. Greed and generosity are mutually exclusive; one can't be both greedy and generous at the same time. Greed is the overwhelming desire to get and keep everything for oneself, and generosity is the overwhelming desire to give and share as much as possible with others. Therefore, teaching people to give and providing an opportunity for them to give is a way of helping them overcome their self-destructive patterns of greed.

John Wesley put it this way: "*Gain all you can* without hurting either yourself or your neighbor. . . . *Save all you can.* . . . *Give all you can.*"[9] If we earn and save well but never learn to give, we stunt our spiritual growth and fail our master who gave himself completely for us.

Giving is ultimately not out of guilt or obligation, but out of gratitude. When we experience gratitude for all that God has done for us, we want to give back to God just to say thanks. Our theme for our annual budget drive is "Count Your Many Blessings," and we use the hymn, "Count your many blessings, name them one by one. Count your many blessings, see what God has done." When people become aware of all the many blessings they have received from God they experience overwhelming gratitude and want to give back to God as a way of expressing that gratitude. As leaders in local congregations, we are blessed to be surrounded by heroes in the sanctuary who give their time, talent, and treasure in order to make a positive difference in the lives of all those around them.

CHAPTER 7

WHEN IT'S TIME TO LEAVE: SMOOTH TRANSITIONS

E. CARVER MCGRIFF

What happens when a large, flourishing church changes senior pastors? Any misstep by the outgoing or the incoming pastor can be disastrous. So, too, do those church members whose judgments influence the larger congregation play a major role in the course of events that follow. This change usually happens for one of two reasons: the presiding pastor moves to another congregation, or the presiding pastor retires. Based on some unhappy case histories, it has been axiomatic that the person who follows a long-time, well-liked pastor will have a short and not particularly pleasing "interim pastorate." That doesn't have to be.

The retirement of pastors from major, growing congregations is happening more and more frequently as pastorates are increasing in duration. Retirement is pretty much a matter of nature's decision. Congregations see it coming. Whereas a bishop's decision to move a pastor may come out of the blue, the retirement is obvious, give or take a year or two. This gives the soon-to-retire pastor time to do some preparation for the person to follow, and it allows the congregation to process its feelings over a far longer period of time.

People in Methodist churches are influenced in three ways by the policy of short pastorates. One, people don't build enduring personal relationships with a pastor they suspect won't be around long. Two, pastors find it hard to invest in the congregation's future when they know they'll be moving on before too many years. Three, short-term pastors never acquire sufficient clout with their people to be able to effect needed change. Clearly, the bonded relationship between pastor and people is dramatically affected by the prospect of an unlimited association versus one of short duration. And just as clearly, it is in that long-term relationship that a trust level can develop wherein the pastor can accomplish major changes where change is needed. All of this argues for much longer pastorates as a policy to facilitate a resurgence of The United Methodist Church.

Let's consider the change at St. Luke's when I retired to be followed by Kent Millard as a case history of a successful transition. My service as pastor of St. Luke's United Methodist Church in Indianapolis, Indiana, began in 1967. During the years that followed, steady growth marked St. Luke's. The church grew by never less than one hundred members per year but never by as many as 200 members. Worship attendance remained more or less at 50 percent of membership. The staff grew in a slow and healthy way, from two pastors to six full-time and one part-time pastor. A part-time education director was eventually succeeded by a full-time director, who went on to acquire several staff associates. The congregation was primarily business and professional people, but there were many who didn't fit that description. Between 1967 and 1993 there were three major building additions. By 1993, the year of my retirement, membership was approximately 4,400 with attendance, including a singles service on Wednesday evening, at well over 1,900 people.

As the time approached for me to retire, an arrangement was made for an associate pastor, a man well-liked by the congregation, to assume temporary leadership of the congregation so a search committee could begin to seek the right person to become senior pastor. Bishop Woodie W. White had just arrived as Bishop of the Indiana area of The United Methodist Church. He proceeded to make a decision which I believe was exceedingly wise and probably more courageous than I realized at the time. White chose to allow a blue ribbon committee of the congregation to travel wherever they wished throughout the country in a search for the right person to be their pastor. After lengthy and intensive preparation in determining just what qualities they sought, the committee began the process of visiting churches, some in our own area, many outside the state. I also made the decision not to be privy to the search and choosing process, as I consider it inappropriate for a pastor to influence in any way the choice of his or her successor.

So began the process of transition. My input took several forms: pronouncements from the pulpit, comments made to church members in casual conversations, and my counsel to the search committee and to the many church leaders who continued as my extended social network. In preparation for this, I made several important decisions. First, and I believe this is crucial for every departing pastor no matter what the circumstances, *I vowed I would never utter a word of criticism of the person who followed me.* I knew with absolute certainty that any word of criticism would sooner or later make its way out into the community, would prejudice some church members against the new pastor, and would thus harm not only my successor but also would harm the church members who might never be able to completely accept him or her as their pastor. As it happened, I was so impressed with the person who arrived, Kent Millard, that the only possible criticism I could make of Kent is that he is so much better at so many things than am I. But however it might have gone, I asked God to sustain me in that vow.

The departing pastor must keep one thought in mind: Change is inevitable and essential when a new pastor arrives, and the change is not a repudiation of previous leadership. It's called progress. Pulitzer Prize winning author David Maraniss, writing in his biography of football legend Vince Lombardi, put it this way: "In the profession of coaching, there are two essential challenges. One is to build a winning team from scratch, the other is to sustain excellence after a club has reached the top. They are distinct tasks, perhaps equally difficult, but usually requiring different intellectual and psychological skills."[1] That is just as true in the building and leading of a major congregation when leadership must change. By God's grace, Kent arrived with just those different psychological and intellectual skills to lead a fine congregation onward and upward. It's why we each have a contribution to make here.

A second decision was to keep the welfare of St. Luke's Church firmly in my heart. I knew there was a danger that as time passed and as the composition of the church changed, my memories and affection for her could dim. I very much wanted to be allowed continuing association with St. Luke's, but I did not want to descend into being Old-What's-His-Name, hanging around looking woebegone and aimless. I therefore adopted a wait-and-see position, leaving it up to Kent to give me a sign of welcome. That, I realized, would hinge not only on his degree of emotional security but also on how he perceived my support of his pastorate. In the meantime I knew it was important that I stay strictly away.

One issue with which I struggled was that of my own social network. With few exceptions, my many friends are active members of St. Luke's. Some were and are leaders central to the church's everyday life. When they gather they often talk about the church. Nearly always that conversation is positive, but from time to time, a note of dissatisfaction can creep in over some current issue. I was very much aware that a raised eyebrow, a smirk, even a moment of heavy silence on my part could seem a judgment. I knew that if I were to continue my social life with these friends uninterrupted and remain faithful to my vow, I must steel myself to extend that decision not to criticize my successor to include not criticizing his decisions as changes inevitably took place.

This all applied in still another way. Although I was now retired, I still had a wide association with clergy friends, and I don't have to tell my ordained readers that it was not at all uncommon for those friends to ask how Kent was doing. Generally, the question was innocent, but there was an occasion or two when I thought I discerned a bit of anticipation as though in hopes that just maybe things would have been better had the bishop appointed the next person on the appointment list. As I've already said, it was easy to report that things at St. Luke's were going well. But I also realized how essential it is in any circumstance that the retiring or departing pastor be unfailingly loyal in saying nothing which might detract from the new pastor's reputation. This was especially important because Kent was new, having arrived from another area, and his reputation would soon determine many facets to his life in Indiana. Negative comments by his predecessor could be damaging. While many other people would play an important role in this process, I, as the one presumably in close contact with the inner working of the church, would surely know "the latest scoop." I also recalled a truism from my early days as a salesman: "Every knock is a boost." That is, my comments about my successor would tell little about him and a lot about me.

Still another decision which I knew to be important was to announce to my congregation prior to Kent's arrival that I was prevented by church law and by simple good manners from performing any ministerial service for a member of that church from the moment of the arrival of the new pastor. It would be heartbreaking, of course, to say no to the many young people who had looked to me as their pastor since their childhood when asked to preside at their weddings or to baptize their children. It would be equally painful as old friends and longtime members passed away to have to tell their loved ones that I who had served as their pastor for twenty-six years could not perform the funeral service.

Indeed, I was approached by families who pled that surely the new pastor wouldn't mind, and after all one small exception on my part would mean so much to their daughter. Bless their hearts, they couldn't understand that "one small exception" could lead to five other families making the same request because "after all, you did it for the Smiths."

There were exceptions. Certain events had been scheduled prior to the choosing the new pastor. Kent quickly agreed that I should keep those promises. Also, as time passed a few people contacted Kent and asked if I could perform a wedding or a funeral. In those instances, I told Kent I'd beg off unless he, for some reason, actually wanted me to do them. He did on several occasions. Kent was unfailingly gracious at all times in these situations which, among other things, told members of the congregation something about their new pastor. In most cases, however, and they were few, I declined. But the point here is that an outgoing pastor must be scrupulous in these matters. Once the practice of returning for weddings and funerals begins it rarely ends until harm has been done and feelings hurt. And it only makes the new pastor's efforts to take the former pastor's place in the people's hearts more difficult. In any exception the commitment must have the wholehearted support of the new pastor.

Another step I took in preparation for my successor was to have an audit done of our membership. We solicited every member family for its wishes regarding children who had moved, these constituting most of our missing members. We also sent letters to families who had not participated in the church's life over the recent past. In the course of my last year we removed some 600 members from our roles, reducing membership from 4,400 to 3,800, the latter a very lean and accurate membership roster. This is advisable and fair for every pastor to do. Otherwise, when members must finally be removed by Charge Conference action it can appear that those people decided to depart when the new pastor arrived when the truth is otherwise.

Now, lest all the above seem to the reader that I'm presenting myself as a selfless candidate for sainthood, it's time to honestly report that in all of this there was a quid pro quo. The entire process of retiring after all those years, and of remaining close to the St. Luke's community but no longer as their pastor, was wrenching emotionally. Retirement, once the fantasies have given way to reality, is at best a mixed blessing. To drive by the building over which I had presided all those years, where I had come and gone and which, in many ways, bore the mark of my aesthetic preferences, only to realize I'm not particularly welcome there now and I have no part in the very work to which I have given the most important part of my life was painful. To awaken on Sunday morning with no responsibilities should have been a long-awaited pleasure. In some ways it was, but I was finding that every book I read, every movie seen, every memorable encounter in the market place sparked ideas for a sermon, none of which I thought I would ever use. The day would come when I would find a new career, but in the early going there was grief and a very definite feeling of exclusion. The only person who could minister to my pain was Kent Millard.

Kent immediately took a step that endeared him to me. He arranged for us to have lunch and to discuss St. Luke's and to hear my counsel. I have known new pastors to arrive at a new appointment with all sorts of grand ideas for change while knowing nothing at all of the culture of the congregation, nothing of its past and its collective hopes and dreams. It is not uncommon for the new person to want to erase all signs of the old guy as soon as reasonably possible. That wasn't Kent. It was clear from the beginning that he honored the past, made no grand claims for himself, and that he planned not to change what I may have accomplished but instead planned to build on that. The day would, of course, come when Kent's own vision would guide the church in new and innovative ways, but not until he had wisely learned all he could about the past and the present. If I had possessed any private jealousies of this man who was taking over my former life they would have disappeared in short order.

One of the wise things Kent did was to pay tribute publicly to my years as pastor and to modestly refrain from making any bold predictions about his own plans. Those members who were prepared to resent this new pastor, and there are always a few of those, were totally disarmed. Furthermore, as time went on Kent was never heard to in any way disparage me or my leadership through the past. Had he done so I would soon have heard. It did not take long for the congregation to realize that Kent Millard and Carver McGriff were fast friends. Kent frequently declared this and was often quoted to me as saying that he counted on me for counsel as he made his way through the early days at St. Luke's. Needless to say, I was more than ready to do anything I could to enable him from afar.

Before long Kent invited me to preach at St. Luke's. I enthusiastically agreed, and we both realized this was the best possible way to cement in people's minds the bond which had grown between the two of us. It wasn't long before my affirming and complimentary comments about Kent were the result of genuine regard, not just the keeping of a vow. In the years since, I have preached there many times and have taught a short-term class on theology. Kent has publicized a couple of my books from his pulpit, and in every way he has gone the extra mile to welcome me and to allow me to feel that I am and will always be part of St. Luke's Methodist Church. As the years have gone by I have made it a point to affirm the new ideas which have resulted from Kent's ministry, another effort made easy by the fact that they are all good ideas. Of course the bottom line in this personal transition was the fact that Kent Millard brought with him all the gifts of person and ministry which have made him effective as pastor of a large and growing church.

To generalize about the transition from one pastor to another no matter the reason for the change, two elements stand out. First, the outgoing pastor must leave with the congregation believing he or she is happy with what is happening even though sad to leave a longtime association of loving relationship, pastor and people, but constantly affirming without criticism or complaint the one who follows. Second, the incoming pastor must sincerely, without criticism or complaint, affirm the former pastor and that person's work. Both must deflect all criticism from parishioners without judgment. If the people see a bond between the two, see evidence that both are making every effort to live out the spirit of Jesus Christ whose name they presume to declare before others, are one in that spirit, brothers, sisters, brother and sister in the faith, the congregation will quickly and easily make the transition themselves, and God will be praised.

Reflections on Chapter 7

M . KENT MILLARD

Carver McGriff has written about his experience in retiring from St. Luke's after serving as senior pastor for twenty-six years and what he did in preparing for his successor. What Carver did has been extremely significant in helping to make a smooth transition from one senior pastor to the next, and is good advice for every pastor who is moving from a dearly loved congregation to another church or into retirement. I would like to share my experience of the transition and the spiritual growth opportunities I had in coming to St. Luke's as its new senior pastor in 1993.

I was in my sixth year of serving as senior pastor of First United Methodist Church in Sioux Falls, South Dakota, when Bishop Woodie White of Indiana called. He began the conversation by saying, "Kent I'd like to disrupt your day." I thought to myself, "He's not my Bishop; my Bishop can disrupt my day but how can a Bishop from Indiana disrupt my day?" I had served various-size-congregations in Massachusetts and South Dakota for twenty-six years and had planned to serve in Sioux Falls First Church for the duration of my ministry. But it seems that God and Bishop White had other plans.

Bishop White had consulted my bishop in South Dakota and was given permission to ask me if I would consider putting my name on a list of pastors being considered for appointment to St. Luke's United Methodist Church in Indianapolis, the largest United Methodist membership congregation in the upper Midwest. He told me that I would be following Dr. Carver McGriff, a much beloved pastor who had served the church for twenty-six years and built it from 900 members to around 4,000 members. He called at noon and wanted an answer by six o'clock that evening. I consulted with my wife and a couple of good friends, and they gave the same advice, "Yes, put your name on the list. It would be an honor to be considered for such an important congregation, but don't go! You'd likely be a short-term interim pastor following such a popular long-term pastor."

Consequently, I called Bishop White and told him I would be willing to be put on the list, and then I went on a trip to Japan and China with our son, who was teaching in Japan at the time. When I returned home, two laymen from St. Luke's called to see if they could come to hear me preach and visit with me about St. Luke's, and I invited them to come. This is not the usual United Methodist way of making appointments, and in hindsight, this may be one of the reasons why my appointment to St. Luke's following a long-term pastor was not a short-term interim pastorate. After visiting with these two active and outstanding laypersons, it became clear to me that the laity of St. Luke's were passionate about their congregation and wanted to do all they could to ensure its continued growth after a dearly loved pastor left. I suspect that there are many passionate lay leaders in all congregations who are left out of the loop when pastoral assignments are made and, consequently, have little invested in the success of the next pastor because they weren't included in the decision.

However, after thinking about this decision for a couple weeks, I decided to say "No." I was still excited about my ministry at First United Methodist Church in Sioux Falls and had been sufficiently warned about the dangers of following a beloved long-term pastor. Usually it is very difficult for a United Methodist pastor to decline an appointment offered by a bishop, but when a pastor is asked to take an appointment in another conference, one can decline much more easily. Nonetheless, one of the laymen who visited me called and told me that they had read an article I once wrote about discerning the will of God. It was an article based on my Doctor of Ministry dissertation in which I maintained that in order to discern God's will you first need to get all the facts you can about the issue under consideration, then look at what the Bible and our faith tradition have to say about the issue and then make your decision in prayer. He said, "You haven't looked at all the facts about St. Luke's. You haven't seen the church and all of its ministries. You might be saying no to what God is calling you to do." I thought, "It's awful when they quote your own writings to you!" Consequently, we agreed to visit St. Luke's before we declined.

Bishop Rueben Job has been a guide and mentor to me for several years, so I visited him to seek some guidance and wisdom about this decision. Bishop Job told me that whenever he faced a vocational crossroads, he always tried to take the path where there was the shadow of the cross. By that he meant to take the path that has the most risk to it, makes you most vulnerable, and makes you depend on God for effectiveness. Now, personally, I was tempted to take the path that had least risk, made me less vulnerable, and was something I felt I could accomplish by my own gifts and power. It became clear to me that staying in Sioux Falls had the least risk to it and going to St. Luke's in Indianapolis and following a very effective long-term senior pastor had the greatest risk associated with it and would make me more dependent on God for effectiveness in this new appointment. However, I realized that I would have a hard time ever asking laypersons to take a risk for the faith or to become vulnerable if, when it came down to it, I couldn't do it myself.

I suspect that most of us are reluctant to take the path where there is the "shadow of the cross." However, I have discovered that God is very faithful; when God calls, God empowers. God is not so much interested in our ability as our availability, and when we make ourselves available to God, God confounds the conventional wisdom of the world and works miracles, like enabling a pastor to effectively follow a long-term pastor who retires and stays in the community. I encourage pastors and laypersons to ask where there is the "shadow of the cross" in their lives and to discover the thrill of surrendering to God and experiencing God's power and wisdom leading us through what others might think to be impossible.

In the past whenever we had been asked to move to a new congregation, I usually said, "Yes, it will be a new opportunity for service," and my wife, Minnietta, would be reluctant to leave our current home saying, "But what about our family and friends we're leaving behind?" However, when the opportunity to move to Indianapolis came up, Minnietta said, "Yes, it will be an exciting new opportunity for service," and I said, "But what about our family and friends we're leaving behind?" We had just reversed roles!

After visiting Bishop White and some of the leaders of St. Luke's, I still had a hard time making a final decision. I listed all the pros and cons of leaving a congregation and annual conference I loved and coming to a new conference where I didn't know any of the pastors and to a new congregation with considerable risk associated with it. I called friends and asked them to pray with me over the phone to help me find God's guidance in this important decision, but I was absolutely torn and didn't know what to do. I went for a walk near the hotel where we were staying and found myself in a small park with a grassy knoll. I knelt down at that knoll and began to pray for God's guidance. I was reminded of Jesus praying in the Garden of Gethsemane, so I began to pray the prayer he prayed, "Lord, let this cup pass from me. Nevertheless, not my will but Thine be done." As I prayed this prayer over and over, the words of *Jesus Christ Superstar* came to me. In the Gethsemane scene, Jesus prays "God your will is hard, but you hold every card...take me now before I change my mind." I prayed "not my will but Thine be done and take me now before I change my mind" over and over, and a peace came over me that is hard to describe, and I knew that I should let the Lord "take me" and we should accept the appointment to St. Luke's.

I returned to the hotel and told my wife that I felt God was calling us to St. Luke's, and that evening we were introduced by Bishop White to the Staff-Parish Relations committee as their new senior pastor and interviewed by the committee. For me it felt like a huge leap of faith, and at the same time I was excited about this new opportunity for ministry and service in one of the most exciting congregations in the nation.

The first person I wanted to meet after accepting this appointment was Carver McGriff, so we went to dinner together. I have huge appreciation and respect for Carver and all that he has done to grow St. Luke's from 900 members when he came in 1967 to nearly 4,000 members when he retired. I had been pastor of a large congregation in South Dakota, and I know firsthand the challenges involved in leading a large staff and congregation.

Carver was extremely gracious in welcoming me and offering his support as I began ministry in this new congregation. He was very helpful in answering my questions about the history, culture, mission, values, and personalities of the congregation God had called me to serve. Carver and I began to meet regularly for breakfast, and he has become a very valuable mentor, counselor, and guide for me in this congregation, and we continue to meet regularly and talk about the congregation. As we became friends, I realized that many new pastors tend to see their predecessor as their enemy and to see themselves as the savior of the congregation and the one who has to "fix" all the things they feel their predecessor did wrong. How foolish! I discovered that Carver was not my enemy; Carver was my best ally and strongest supporter as I began my ministry here and as it has continued.

Several months after I arrived, I invited Carver back to preach one Sunday morning. I told the congregation that while Carver and I are different in many ways, we still have the same goal. Carver doesn't want to build a congregation to 4,000 members and then watch it fall apart after he leaves, and I don't want to come to a large congregation and see it fall apart because I came! Both of us want to see St. Luke's continue to grow in faithfulness and effectiveness, and both of us are committed to doing what we can to help that growth. I have invited Carver to return about once each year to help us with some particular aspect of ministry. Once he came to speak to a large group about the need for our new expansion project, and I know that many people, who had reservations about the capital project, were enrolled in it because of Carver's endorsement. Carver has also returned for fundraising dinners, groundbreaking ceremonies, church founders recognition dinners, our fiftieth anniversary celebration, and to preach when I am on vacation or on sabbatical.

I suspect the biggest conflict that occurs between pastors and their predecessors centers on the conducting of weddings and funerals. On the one hand, a family who has been close to a particular pastor often wants that pastor to conduct the wedding or funeral service for their family members. On the other hand, the new pastor wants to conduct the wedding or funeral because he or she is now the pastor in charge and this will give the new pastor an opportunity to develop a pastoral relationship with the family.

Before he retired, Carver made it clear to the congregation that he would not be available for weddings and funerals because he was no longer the pastor of the congregation. However, there have been several occasions where, as I visit with a family about a funeral particularly, I discover they have a special bond with Carver and I ask if they would like for him to participate in the service and they feel relieved that I not only allow but encourage Carver to participate. On one occasion, a founding member, who had been one of Carver's closest friends, passed away; so it seemed most appropriate for Carver to give the homily for the funeral service, and the family was overwhelmingly grateful. Our goal is to work together to help grieving persons through their time of grief and loss and not to defend turf or egos. Usually, I or one of the other pastors on staff will work with the family in preparing and leading a funeral service, and Carver will give the eulogy. Countless members of the congregation have told us both how much it means to them to see pastors working together rather than criticizing each other or excluding each other as so often happens.

Pastors may give marvelous sermons about love, forgiveness, teamwork, and reconciliation, but if they cannot demonstrate those qualities in their attitudes and actions toward their prede- cessor, their words from the pulpit will not be credible.

When a new pastor comes, some members of the congregation will seek to win points with the new pastor by telling them how much better they are than their predecessor in some area of min- istry. Whenever someone says something that implies a criticism of Carver, I always respond by simply saying that Carver is my friend and I have nothing but deep respect and admiration for his ministry at St. Luke's. I also remind people that each pastor is dif- ferent and brings different gifts to the leadership of the congrega- tion and when I leave here, my successor will undoubtedly have strengths I don't have and will lead the congregation in some new ways as well.

The truth of the matter is that the current pastor sets the tone in the relationship with a former pastor. If the current pastor has self-knowledge and is secure in his or her own relationship with God and the congregation, then the new pastor will want to enroll the predecessor in the new vision for the congregation and utilize the former pastor's strengths, endorsements, and relationships to help the congregation move forward. In the fifty-year history of St. Luke's, there have only been four senior pastors. The Reverend Bill Imler was the founding pastor and served here for six years, Dr. Richard Hamilton succeeded him and served here for eight years, and Dr. Carver McGriff succeeded him and served here for twenty-six years, or for more than half of the life of this congregation. We have invited all of the senior pastors back for special occasions, and the congregation has been blessed by their return and ministry among us.

I would like to make one final comment regarding a smooth transition between pastors. Carver retired in June 1993, and I did not come to the church until October, 1993, which means there was a four-month interim time between senior pastors. St. Luke's has always been blessed with very competent associate pastors, and they led the church very well during the interim. However, I believe that having an interim time between Carver's leaving and my arriving was very important to our smooth transition. I believe that any new pastor who had come the week following Carver's retirement would have had a difficult time. People needed time to grieve the loss of a dearly loved pastor. When someone loses a spouse they need time to grieve that loss before they are ready for any new relationship. In a similar way, when a congregation loses a dearly loved pastor, they need time and space to grieve that loss before they are ready for a new relationship with any new pastor. Bishops and cabinets would do well to give congregations some time to grieve the loss of a dearly loved pastor before sending in a new pastor. It may well be that one of the reasons why there are so many short, unhappy interim situations following a long-term pastor is because there has been no time allowed for the grief process to work itself out before a new pastor is sent in.

Our prayer for those who read these words is that God would use them to encourage every local church pastor and lay leader to recognize the spark of God in every person, to fan that spark into flame, and to allow God to set the world on fire with the good news of God's unconditional love in Jesus Christ.

NOTES

1. What in the World *Is a Passion Driven Church?*

1. Lyle Schaller, *Tattered Trust: Is There Hope for Your Denomination?* (Nashville: Abingdon Press, 1996), 90-91.

2. Paul Tournier, *The Meaning of Persons* (New York: Harper & Row, 1957), 42.

3. Robert D. Putnam, *Bowling Alone: The Collapse and Revival of American Community* (New York: Simon & Schuster, 2000), 66-67.

4. Ibid.

2. *Passion Inspired Leaders*

1. Stephen R. Covey, *The Seven Habits of Highly Effective People* (New York: Simon & Schuster, 1989), 101.

2. Bruce Larson, *The Whole Christian* (Waco: Word Books, 1983), 92-93.

3. John C. Maxwell, *Developing the Leaders Around You* (Nashville: Thomas Nelson, 1995), 28.

4. Covey, *Seven Habits of Highly Effective People*, 187.

5. Brewer Mattocks in *Minister's Prayer Book*, ed. John Doberstein (Philadelphia: Fortress Press, 1986), 359.

6. Richard Warren, *The Purpose Driven Church: Growth Without Compromising Your Message and Mission* (Grand Rapids, Mich.: Zondervan, 1955), 39.

7. Questions about permission to use this quotation should be directed to Charles Powell at topten@coachville.com

3. Successful Team Building

1. Dale Carnegie, *How to Win Friends and Influence People* (New York: Pocket Books, 1936; rev. 1981), 23.
2. Tournier, *The Meaning of Persons*, 38.
3. Amy Joyce, "Office Politics with a Teenage Twist: Co-Worker Cliques Have Their Advantages—Unless You're on the Outside," *The Washington Post*, 10 March 2002, sec. F, p. H6.
4. Ibid.
5. William James in *How to Win Friends and Influence People*, 18.

4. Sunday at Eleven, and All Those Other Services

1. Warren Hartman and Robert L. Wilson, *The Large Membership Church* (Nashville: Discipleship Resources, 1989), 19.
2. Phillips Brooks, *Lecture on Preaching* (Grand Rapids: Zondervan, n.d.), 5, 6.
3. Schaller, *Tattered Trust*, 24-25.
4. John Shelby Spong, *A New Christianity for a New World: Why Traditional Faith Is Dying and How a New Faith Is Being Born* (San Francisco: HarperSanFrancisco, 2001), 254.
5. Sydney Smith, from "Lady Holland's Memoir" in *Familiar Quotations*, comp. John Bartlett (Boston: Little, Brown, & Co., 1955), 418.
6. Anne Lamott, *Traveling Mercies: Some Thoughts on Faith* (New York: Pantheon Books, 1999), 60.
7. Richard J. Foster, *Celebration of Discipline: The Path to Spiritual Growth* (San Francisco: HarperSanFrancisco, 1978), 139.
8. Ibid., 138.
9. Ibid., 139.

5. Compassionate Change

1. Lyle Schaller, *Strategies for Change* (Nashville: Abingdon Press, 1993), 10.
2. Covey, *Seven Habits of Highly Effective People*, 241.
3. Dale Carnegie, *How to Win Friends and Influence People*, 110.
4. Danny E. Morris and Charles M. Olson, *Discerning God's Will Together: A Spiritual Practice for the Church* (Nashville: Upper Room Books, 1997), 135, from Danny E. Morris, *Yearning to Know God's Will* (Grand Rapids, Mich.: Zondervan, 1991), 106.
5. Charles de Foucauld, *Meditations of a Hermit* (New York: Orbis Books, 1981).
6. John Wesley, "A Covenant Prayer in the Wesleyan Tradition," *The United Methodist Hymnal* (Nashville: The United Methodist Publishing House, 1989), 607.

6. Heroes in the Sanctuary

1. Theodore Roosevelt, *Familiar Quotations*, 778.
2. Cecil Francis Alexander, "Jesus Calls Us," 1852.

3. J. W. Stevenson, *God in My Unbelief* (London: Collins-St. James Place, 1960), 57.

4. Peter Gomes, *The Good Life: Truths That Last in Times of Need* (San Francisco: HarperSanFrancisco, 2002), 29.

5. Lyle Schaller, *44 Ways to Increase Church Attendance* (Nashville: Abingdon Press, 1988), 24.

6. Bernard Towers, *Teilhard de Chardin* (Richmond: John Knox Press, 1966), 39.

7. Stevenson, *God in My Unbelief*, 14.

8. Albert C. Outler, ed., *Sermons II 34-70*, vol 2 of *The Works of John Wesley* (Nashville: Abingdon Press, 1985), 278-79.

7. When It's Time to Leave: Smooth Transitions

1. David Maraniss, *When Pride Still Mattered: A Life of Vince Lombardi* (New York: Simon & Schuster, 1999), 136.